Praise for *Breaking Up with Busy*

"Yvonne Tally delivers her message with a light hand and a sense of humor, making hers a voice that people trust and find inspiring."
— *Kat Gordon,* founder of the 3% International Conference

"Yvonne Tally's energy is boundless, and her clients wish they could buy a bottle of it. With this book, now they can!"
— *Robbie Baxter,* author of *The Membership Economy* and founder of Peninsula Strategies

"As a consumer reporter, I have done countless stories on the next best thing to get in shape and get healthy. I have heard it all and done it all! But what I never had done before was exercise and train my mind to work in a productive and positive way to change my most challenging habits. Working with Yvonne Tally has helped me create a new way of thinking and living. It is one of the most powerful things I have ever done."
— *Jeanette Pavini,* two-time Emmy Award–winning journalist and coauthor of *Raising Baby Green*

"Yvonne Tally seems to have unlocked the secret formula for a truly balanced and mindful approach that addresses our inner sense of calm, presence, and well-being. I have shared her intuitive, highly effective, groundbreaking method with entire families, and it works. Today, tomorrow, and for years to come, it works."
— *Dave Grandin,* MFCC therapist

"What a refreshing and deeply useful guide to busting your stories and beliefs about why you *must* be so very busy. I made tons of notes and immediately implemented several ideas. But most of all? I felt far less alone in my busyness and more willing to do something about it. This is one of those books you'll want to revisit again and again as you change your story about busy."
— *Jennifer Louden,* author of *The Life Organizer* and *The Woman's Comfort Book*

Breaking Up with

BUSY

Breaking Up with

BUSY

REAL-LIFE SOLUTIONS
FOR OVERSCHEDULED WOMEN

YVONNE TALLY

New World Library
Novato, California

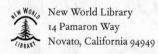

 New World Library
14 Pamaron Way
Novato, California 94949

Copyright © 2018 by Yvonne Tally

Text design by Tona Pearce Myers

Library of Congress Cataloging-in-Publication data is available.

First printing, April 2018
ISBN 978-1-60868-525-7
Ebook ISBN 978-1-60868-526-4
Printed in Canada on 100% postconsumer-waste recycled paper

New World Library is proud to be a Gold Certified Environmentally Responsible Publisher. Publisher certification awarded by Green Press Initiative. www.greenpressinitiative.org

10   9   8   7   6   5   4   3   2   1

To my sweet daughter, Juliette.
In everything that love is, you are. xoxo

Contents

Introduction

"I'm busy" has become the new "I'm fine," a chant heard everywhere, from the sidelines of soccer games to the hallways of offices. There is a cultural expectation that women should always be busy, and if they're not, well, they must not be all that important, or worse, they must be lazy.

Busyness is not just a behavior; it is an ethos that claims ownership of our time. Moving away from busy behavior takes more than just solutions; it requires each of us to discover the motivation underneath our behavior. That's the only way we will stop the endless overscheduling and the side-eyeing of our fellow sisters when we see them not being "busy enough." As soon as we understand what's driving our behavior, we'll be able to make changes and reclaim our leisure time rather than simply giving it away.

Busy is an odd status symbol. It is like fake designer clothing — it looks really good from the outside, but on the inside the structure is uneven, details are missing, and only the wearer knows that what others see is an illusion. For many this ruse provides a sense of fitting in to an elite group. And don't we all want to fit in? It's human nature to want to belong and to feel our contributions are being valued. But what price are we paying to be a part of this busy group? And how did being busy go from being a pastime to a lifestyle?

The Overscheduled Woman (OSW) knows all too well what being busy feels like. For her the "I'm busy" refrain is all too accurate. As she time-slices through her days, trying to keep up with all the demands, busy is setting the pace. What would help? A clone, an assistant, a vacation? Yes, as a matter of fact, all three are exactly what she needs to get busy off her schedule. But without the use of a helpful robot or a hands-free voice-activated virtual assistant, she's on her own, long to-do list in one hand and cell phone blowing up in the other. A screenshot of her days reveals a variety pack of demands and requests: *Where are you? I need this... You're late for... Hey, can you also pick up... I need that report done, stat! You're already booked at that time. Mom, why haven't you answered my text? Honey, where are my... I've started the meeting — when will you be here? Your reservation was canceled; you were too late!* The list of texts, emails, and missed phone calls rips through her busy days with the precision of an X-Acto knife, swift, deep, and without mercy.

How is the OSW supposed to make it all fit together and still find a little *me* time? Is that asking too much? How will she know when she's on the edge of that notorious rabbit hole, ready to slip into the abyss of busyness? Unfortunately, the OSW is so busy she often misses the signs, free-falling into that overscheduled lifestyle, and before she knows it, her busy tempo is her new normal. However, if she's lucky, something will show up before she takes the final tumble, a push sufficient to wake her up but not enough to make her fall headfirst.

For me, that *push* happened on a beautiful August morning: mascara in hand, coffee set to one side of my makeup mirror, as my world suddenly went black. Stars flying, vision blurring, heart racing, chest seizing, right there in my bathroom. I collapsed to the floor and desperately tried to breathe.

I thought I was having a heart attack, and with that realization, my panic of losing everything I loved set in. I instantly counted all the people in my life who depended on me. How could I let them down like this? How could this be happening to me? Was I going to die right there on my bathroom floor?

The paramedics arrived, and as they administered oxygen to my mid-made-up face, my vanity surfaced. I thought about my messy bedroom, the breakfast dishes stacked in the sink, and the one eye that still had no mascara. These were clear signs that my priorities were severely out of whack. How could I be thinking about not being perfectly pulled together at a time like this?

Loaded into the ambulance and on my way to the hospital, all I could think was, *Not now, I have too much to do!* After a battery of tests, and several hours of waiting for results, the emergency room doctor announced I had not had a heart attack. Looking over the top of his glasses, he declared, "You've had a panic attack." Me? A panic attack? Surely, he's got the wrong report! I felt embarrassed. And when he followed with, "This happens to women all the time," I was insulted yet curious. How had I missed the signs? Was I in denial about my life slipping off its well-organized rails? I had repeatedly excused my frustrations and irritability as normal, because it all had become so normal. The rushing, the overplanning, the overscheduling, the commitments, events, and obligations: they all began to unfurl in front of me. I was blindsided by my own busyness. I was ashamed, annoyed, and downright determined to make some changes. I didn't have the time, or the money, to be taking trips to the hospital or waiting in an emergency room on a gurney seeing other people with real emergencies. It was time for a *me intervention*. In the moment after the doctor said, "It happens..." I promised myself I would not let it happen again. I didn't know how I would stop the madness, but I was determined to find a way.

I decided to take a closer look at what was generating so much angst and tension in my life. I was perplexed as to how someone like me — a positive-thinking, active, organic-eating exerciser — could end up in the back of an ambulance.

As my curiosity took flight, and I shared my experience with other women, I was astounded at how many of them had similar stories. Numerous women described feeling overwhelmed and had experienced panic attacks, fatigue, chronic frustrations and irritability, depression, and the occasional meltdown behind the closed doors of their offices and bathrooms. The mix included women who seemed to have it together, getting their *stuff done* and making it look seamless, appearing to effortlessly balance their careers with their personal lives. These women were the highly motivated and successful women in the room, the best PTA parents, community volunteers, and organizers of social and corporate events. They were the first ones on the block to have their holiday shopping done, spring garden planted, and family summer vacation planned by the first of January every year. They were the ones who sailed through college with wit and determination, built a career in which they excelled, balanced everything with a zesty social life and skilled execution, both in the boardroom and in their private enclave of home and family — or so it appeared. They were overscheduled, and I needed to figure out a solution to help all of them, myself included.

The solutions were at my fingertips, but I had been so busy in my relationship with busy that I didn't even realize I had become the proverbial cobbler without any shoes. I had spent more than twenty years sharing my techniques for living a healthy lifestyle, and yet I was ignoring a big piece of that prescription: mindfulness.

Mindfulness is more than just having a good attitude, and I sensed there was a way I could connect it with the positive impacts that fitness and healthful food offered. Everyone knows how important both are, but for some reason, until recently mindfulness has not been as fully accepted as a tool for transforming one's life.

As I turned my attention to making that connection, I recalled an experience I had had with my mother some twenty years earlier. It was Mother's Day weekend, and she had invited me to go to a Neurolinguistic Programming (NLP) seminar. It was a small group of about fifty, all looking for ways to improve the quality of their daily lives or to help their clients do the same. The presenter was dynamic, charming, and a powerfully poignant speaker. When he asked for a volunteer from the audience, I raised my hand. Why, I don't know; that wasn't something I liked to do — to be exposed in front of a bunch of people I didn't know. Nonetheless, I went up on the stage and took my place on the stool provided.

The technique he said he would guide me through was a method of releasing emotional disturbances from my subconscious. Great. Just what I wanted: to cry in front of a roomful of strangers.

As he directed me through a series of questions, I answered each, surprised at my candor. However, about midway through, I felt my entire body tense up with emotion. My palms got sweaty, my forehead tightened, my cheeks turned hot and red, and I could feel my eyes begin to sting. Just as my tear faucet was about to open, he abruptly said, "Repeat your phone number backward!" What? Was this guy crazy? I'm thinking, *I was just getting ready to have a good cry over those crummy memories you helped me stir up, and now you want me to do* what?

As I struggled to see the numbers in my head backward and repeat them out loud, I felt my body begin to calm down. My cheeks were no longer steaming, and all signs of tears were gone. The exercise of repeating my phone number backward initiated a conscious pause from the emotions attached to my story.

It's like driving along the same road every day without thinking about the next turn. It's all so familiar and predictable. And then one day, out of nowhere, a child dashes in front of your car. You slam on your brakes, and instantly you're aware of your surroundings. Whatever you may have been thinking is gone, and all your attention is on the unexpected event — the present moment. Repeating my phone number worked in the same way. It's a quick yet simple method to shift from unresourceful automatic thinking to the reality of the present moment.

That day I realized I often functioned from a subconscious level of reactions that I had long ago built, that my past experiences — my training — developed my habits and led my emotions. And although the technique that day was just a small and partial sample of NLP, it altered my awareness. I was instantaneously struck by the powerful possibilities this training could offer and all the techniques that help uncover limiting behaviors and unresourceful habits. Still, I wasn't quite ready to be honest with myself, and it would take another twenty years, and that panic attack, to get me there.

In 2012, after that panic attack, I pursued and acquired my NLP Master Practitioner credentials. And thanks to Tim and Kris Hallbom of the NLP Institute of California, my training set me on an accelerated path for making swift and lasting lifestyle changes.

I set out to chronicle the habits leading to the frustrations of a time-strapped lifestyle. What I found is that it's not just habits creating busy behavior; there is also an underlying ethos whispering, *Women said they could do it all, so they got it all* — *all* meaning family and career, and we have been doing both for the past four decades at a pace that has put us squarely on the main street of Busy Town. The price we've paid to run this race includes career delays and interruptions, limited extended family support, more financial responsibilities, and even more societal expectations that we should do it all, and well. And if we don't *get it all done* without losing our cool or hiding out in the backseats of our cars to steal a few minutes of alone time, we sense that we have failed.

My panic attack was a symptom of my hectic lifestyle. My day began at 4:45 AM, after I had napped intermittently through the night, racking up about five hours of sleep. My work day typically lasted twelve hours and often continued late at night after my young daughter went to bed. And although I loved what I was doing, I was doing too much. My lifestyle included regular fitness and healthy eating; however, my habit of overscheduling began to outweigh the benefits of both. It was that not-so-gentle push that I needed to make some habit-changing choices. I had to find solutions, and I did. Those solutions and practices are what you will find in this book.

I'm happy to say I haven't had a panic attack since I uncovered my brand of busy and worked through each of the solutions outlined in this book. I have developed each technique using my experience and those of the women I have had the pleasure to work with for more than twenty years. I have been greatly inspired by the work of Deepak Chopra, Jack Kornfield, Rick Hanson, and Sondra Kornblatt. Their brilliant books have had a great impact on the fields of mindfulness, science, and lifestyle.

This book is a culmination of my work using my Fitness-Food-Attitude approach and my Five-Step Super Solutions Process. These, along with NLP-inspired techniques, form the foundation of the solutions for breaking up with busy. Your aspirations, goals, and personal time don't deserve to be relegated to the optional column of your day. No, you deserve better, and as a fellow Over-scheduled Woman, I wrote this book to give you a way out of your busy traps and a path back to living the life you desire.

If you're one of the 55 million women struggling to reclaim your days, without the flurry of hustle and rush, your first step out of the busy race is to stop and take a break. This book gives you an effective — and fun — process for bringing back your brand of well-deserved enjoyment and calm. You'll decrease the hurried frenzy of *getting it all done* and learn to lighten up on yourself and to reassess your expectations. You'll learn the signs that lead to your busy pace, what type of OSW you are, how to reset your mind-set, and the busy-busting solutions that are best suited for your breakup with busy. You'll support your transformation using my Five-Step Super Solutions Process and perhaps make it your go-to tool for dropping your busy habits. Each solution can be quickly mastered so that no matter what situation you are faced with, you can tap into your personal power and transform your time — immediately! And to keep you on your busy-free path, the playbook is filled with fifty-two refreshers and reminders that will carry you through each week. This book will be your magic wand, your golden ticket, and your secret sauce.

Women today have reset the bar, and it's high. We expect our performance to be flawless and our energy endless, undertaking multiple roles that will set us apart from the ordinary. We collectively aim to be the most creative and dynamic professionals, the parents with all the answers, the most understanding and loving partners, and the best and most reliable friends. Our perfectionistic expectations have led to this unrealistic and terribly demanding mind-set, and we multitask from one event to another, silently murmuring under our exhausted coffee-soaked breath, *Something's got to give, and I'm tired of it always being me!* It's time to change that paradigm and begin moving in a new direction, one step at a time.

I ask you, just for a moment, to suspend all judgment, all assumptions, and to think of your one-step-at-a-time as a waterfall streaming from the center of a beautiful mountain. A cascading waterfall doesn't start by being a waterfall; it begins with a single droplet of rain. Its magnificence and power lie within its connectedness, not its separateness. Your connection with self is similar to the waterfall; you are a magnificent creation of your mind and body, your spirit and soul. It's time to reconnect each and be whole again, as you are meant to be.

The women who are a part of our lives are uniquely affected by our overscheduled lifestyles. Unknowingly, we are manufacturing a stamp of approval for other women to do the same, and we are imparting this overscheduled mind-set to the next generation of women. As you step forward into your light, you lay the path for these other women to follow. Together, we can change the paradigm of what *having it all* means, and in the process, establish a juggernaut of change, so that every woman finds herself to be enough. Breaking up with busy is the first step.

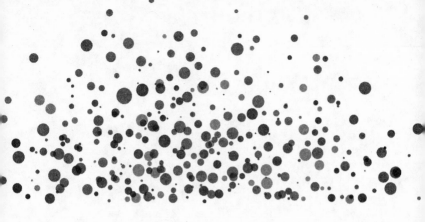

PART ONE

Breaking Up with

BUSY

CHAPTER ONE

Confessions of an Overscheduled Woman

If you are an overscheduled woman, you possess Superwoman-like powers that leave others scratching their heads as to how you get so much done. Sans the magic, bulletproof cuffs on your wrists, you have a knack for juggling many balls at a time without breaking an obvious sweat. You're highly motivated and committed to being the best you can be, as often as possible. You may be an alpha with an uncanny sense of when to encourage others to shine. Or an optimist with the enthusiasm of a popular sorority sister and a visionary's capacity to lead others. You may be a perfectionist and like to please others, a team player as much as an independent thinker, but there's one thing for sure: you're busy!

As an OSW you may be everything from a well-intended problem-solver to a driven and tireless overdeliverer. Both can be personal assets as well as professional attributes; however, an excess of either will wear you down. When this happens, all the signs of busy light up like a Las Vegas marquee.

• *Match Made in a Hurry* •

Being overscheduled goes together with being busy; it's a match made in a hurry. Hundreds of clients have shared with me their stories and their unusually creative methods for keeping up with their lives. At first glance, their particular busy habits may seem easy to change. However, the *get-it-done* attitude that makes the busy ethos so widely accepted is deeply embedded in the OSW ideology.

● OSW Confession: Eating Meals on the Go

I take my frozen Jenny Craig meal out of the freezer in the morning, and while I'm running errands, it sits on the dashboard of my car. By noon it is thawed out and warm enough to eat. It fits right in my lap, so I can continue driving to where I need to get to without stopping somewhere to eat!

Busyness has gone from taking over a few minutes of each day to swallowing the day whole. Once a seemingly innocuous habit, busyness is now a culture, an addictive attraction promising the opportunity to fit in, get ahead, and be the best.

Access to higher education, employment, and flexible motherhood choices don't automatically equal freedom; rather, they are often a gateway to meetings that can't be missed, promises that can't be kept, and schedules that blur the lines between one day and the next. All sorts of corner cutting, which we do just to make things work, eats away at any free time. The imbalance between obligation and expectation results in making personal replenishment a mere footnote to the day, at best.

● OSW Confession: "I Stunk at Being a Room Parent"

My daughter really wanted me to be her room parent, and I really wanted to do it for her, but my job is so demanding that I didn't know if I could make the time. When I asked another mom in the class to share the role with me, she responded, "That never works. Besides, you should get your priorities straight; your daughter is not going to be this age forever." I felt like I had been kicked out of a group I didn't even know I was in. I ended up taking on the room parent job, and I failed miserably. Luckily, my sister went to most of the in-classroom events, but it's something I've always felt bad about; I should have found a way to be there. I'm so good at my job and managing a team of really smart people, but getting twenty second-graders to the science museum escaped me.

| *I'm busier than a one-legged tap dancer!*

• *The Road to Overscheduled* •

The promise that staying busy will make you part of an elite pack of doers and changemakers is part of the

OSW's indoctrination to busyness. It's like receiving a wink from an admirer: you feel special but you're not really sure why, or what it means.

Do you find yourself checking off your long list of to-dos while simultaneously making a new list for the next day? Or multitasking even though you know it's not helping you get anything done faster? Getting stuff done and being busy feed our sense that, yes, we are important and, yes, we matter. It may not be a conscious thought; in fact, we may really feel that our busy lifestyles are necessary. They're not. They're exhausting.

As parents, we spend a minimum of eighteen years raising our children so that they can leave for college or elsewhere. And it often doesn't stop there; at least once, while in their twenties, most adult children will boomerang back into their childhood bedrooms that we now claim as our home offices.

As professionals, it takes about the same amount of time to build a successful career. And if you're single and looking for a partner, you may also need to carve out enough time to find a dating site, set up a profile, and then vet, meet, greet, and repeat. It's a process.

If we put all these efforts on a bucket list, it might look something like this: love, career, family. Sounds reasonable enough, right? But read between the lines, and you'll find that's where the trap has been set to keep us dancing the busy dance, on one leg, at double tempo, and with no end to the performance. I'm tired just thinking about what the OSW has planned next.

I love to be part of what's happening. I typically book my commitments back-to-back — I like getting a lot done in a day. But because I work full-time and have two kids, I have to find a way to fit all this in without it running into my family time. Weekends are the toughest because my kids have so many sports activities. Once I had two weddings in one day. I went to the church service of one and the reception of the other, and then back to the first so I could be at the reception. Each wedding was so different that I had to have two dresses. I used my Houdini skills to change in the car. I thought it was funny, but my husband thought I was nuts! He asked me why we had to go to both. "Because they expected me to be there, and I didn't want to let either of them down!" I said. It didn't seem odd to me at all. I like giving my all and being the best! It's what I do.

And there you have it — the tribal lyrics of the OSW: Make it all happen, get it done, be the best, and give it your all! And then do it again!

My mother used to say, "I'm busier than a one-legged tap dancer." I now get what she meant, and I'm sure you do, too. As you can see from the OSW stories in this chapter, many other women are dancing as fast as they can to keep up with the lives they have set in motion. You will find, as you explore the solutions in this book, that uncovering the motivations underneath your busy behavior and mindfully setting boundaries are both key to making optimal use of your best OSW characteristics. You'll learn how to stop the flow of busy and reset your tempo so you can begin dancing in harmony, not in a hurry.

CHAPTER TWO

The Busy Race and the Price of Your Pace

GINNY'S OSW STORY

Ginny was an on-the-go mom. She had a demanding job that required her to attend several midweek meetings, and she traveled for her job one week each month. Her husband traveled as well, and together they were raising three children, all under the age of ten. On parents' day at her daughter's school, she sent her best friend to stand in for her. "How did your daughter feel about your not being there?" I asked. "It's all about outsourcing. I told her that the stand-in "mom" would be much more fun than me. She understands that Mom is busy and that I can't always be there. I would outsource brushing my teeth if I could!"

If there's one thing I want you to take away from this chapter, it's this: You are living a life, not running a race. Slowing the pace so you're not racing and constantly playing catch-up begins one step at a time. And the first step is to understand what motivates your behavior and the comfort the behavior provides you. Once you do, you can devise some solid solutions and make space for new resourceful habits to take hold.

You'll begin doing that by exploring the Ten Signs That You Need to Break Up with Busy, which will help you determine what's underneath your busy habits. It's time to get in touch with who you are without all that busyness and to begin setting a new pace that feels right for you. In the process, you'll influence other women to do the same.

Ten Signs That You Need to Break Up with Busy

1. You frequently opt out of doing something for yourself when one of your loved ones requests your time.
2. You have a mixed sense of doing too much and not getting enough done.
3. Busy is your new normal.
4. You feel controlled by your schedule.
5. You eat at least one meal each day while standing up or doing something else.
6. You're experiencing weight shifts, skin issues, or hair loss.
7. You're not getting enough sleep, you have insomnia, your libido is low.
8. Things you once enjoyed taking time for now feel like inconveniences.
9. You often feel overwhelmed or anxious.

10. You constantly feel like you are rushing just to keep up with yourself.

Do any of these signs feel familiar? Of course they do! Busy is a club with far too many members. Ignoring these signs may seem harmless enough; however, busyness can put you and your health at risk. Though I could check off most of the items on the list above, like many other OSWs, I ignored the signs until I ended up in the emergency room. Unfortunately, that's not an uncommon event for many women, nor is having a compromised immune system brought on by ignoring our bodies' signals. To get a better understanding of how these symptoms have become so prevalent, let's take a brief yet essential look at how all this busy business got rolling and the impact its pace has on you. Let's begin with Ann's story, an example of how intelligent and successful women still unwittingly ignore their busy signs.

Ann's OSW Story

Ann was a high-achieving and professionally successful OSW. When she was in her midtwenties, she started her first company. She went on to attain her MBA while pregnant with her fourth child. Ann was exceptional in all areas of business but was miserable in her private life. She had a fractured relationship with her parents and spouse, and her children were emotionally distant, even though she had done "everything right" and "everything her parents expected of her," excelling beyond her own stratospheric standards. When she was in her early forties, she began experiencing digestion problems, severe insomnia, and abrupt weight gain. She had seen the finest doctors, and none could diagnose her ailments or connect them to a disease. She was so busy achieving what she felt was expected of her that she lived with these conditions for several years, accepting them as a product of her demanding lifestyle.

The first day she arrived in my office, she brought with her detailed records from the numerous doctors she had seen and her plan for what she wanted me to do. I said to her, "It looks like you have already discovered your solutions. Why are you seeking my help?" Ann responded, "I just want someone to make me do what I know I'm supposed to do." She didn't really want me to be the one in charge; letting someone else make decisions meant relinquishing control, and that would mean trusting uncertainty, something she was not at all comfortable with.

It wasn't until she had worked with me for about six months that she was able to let her guard down enough to begin exploring what was really under her perfectionistic habits. She had been surrounded by very successful women all her life and had watched her mother and aunts go on to achieve super-success. Her own success was never really something she planned; it was just something expected of her. She described feeling like she was always racing to catch up with herself. She wasn't even sure she liked what she was doing. In fact, she had always wanted to be a ballet dancer, not a CEO. Professional success was so familiar, yet she had little confidence in building and developing her personal relationships. The more she tried to control her relationships, the more her loved ones distanced themselves from her, and that in turn fueled her insecurities and kept her from trying a different approach. She also realized her *uncertainties and angsts were being displayed in her physical symptoms.*

These discoveries and her recognition of them initiated a dynamic change. I designed a fitness plan that fit her real life, not one that she was "supposed" to be living. I included daily meditation (that was a hard sell!) as part of her wellness program. We had an agreement that she would eat at least one meal a day sitting down, without her devices and devoid of business conversations. Ann began setting better boundaries at work and making more time for her family. Over time, her physical symptoms began to subside, until they dissipated altogether. It was a slow process; however, her changes stuck.

Ann is still highly successful, and now that includes having a better relationship with her children and her spouse. Her life is not perfect; it's better, and she has finally accepted that better is often her best. As a side note, Ann joined an adult ballet class, just for fun. She has redefined busy, and it is now an exception to her day, not a habit.

As we can see from Ann's story, being busy doesn't happen in a bubble; busy behavior trickles down and ripples out. She learned it from watching the women in her family, and her learned behavior in turn had an impact on her family. The energy of busy behaviors affects everyone with whom you come into contact, and the more time you spend with these people — partners, spouses, children, and coworkers — the larger your impact will be on them.

The big question is, How did busy become such a bully? Pushing and shoving its way into life as though it belongs and is as important as, oh, I don't know, things like love, family, and happiness? But there it is, manipulating time to the point that we're so busy being busy that we feel lazy or guilty when we sit too long at dinner. Oh, but that's right, who am I kidding? Nobody sits down for dinner anymore — we're too busy! The bully of busy cleverly steals our time while promising to give us more. Understanding how busy got so powerful, pervasive, and acceptable will help you begin reclaiming your time and make even more of it.

• The Business of Busy •

Time is like a Ponzi scheme; most of us feel we never get a good return on the investments we've made. Technology has had a profound impact on the illusion of time. Most of us habitually use loads of gadgets, thinking they aid us in freeing up time and space but in reality, they provide a steady stream of distractions. We can Facebook all our "friends" with a few strokes of the keyboard; we can text a conversation and avoid the time-absorbing niceties that are expected in a phone call. We Instagram our daily moments as if we're in a professional photo shoot, with age-enhancing filters and hashtags galore to let the world know that we're important and that we're busy!

Many of us who once considered the implications of our biological clocks are now surrounded by the constant reminders of the clocks on our laptops, tablets, smartphones, and automobiles. The reminders of time are constant and everywhere. Technology and its tantalizing time-saving gadgets have turned us into time wizards, like Willy Wonka conveyor belts, pumping out numerous tasks, appointments, errands, meetings, and chores. And thanks to these techy innovations, we can order food any time of the day and have it dashed to our doors; we can date, via the internet, while eating a bowl of ice cream in our PJs at 2:00 PM on a Sunday; heck, we can even file for divorce, pay taxes, and find a relative living in a cave somewhere in South America without ever leaving our backyard chaise lounge. We can have almost anything we want whenever we want it — and therein lies the problem. Busyness has no boundaries, with its unlimited self-imposed demands steeped in a myriad of expectations.

Busy goes far beyond the use of technology and our addictive draw to it. The feeling of being rushed and out of time has become embedded in our get-it-done culture. As economies grow and incomes rise, we have attached a financial value on time — it's worth more. We negotiate with ourselves over the use of our time, as though we have to ask permission to spend time the way we want. The less time we have, the more we want, and so go the hands around the clock — ticktock, ticktock, until we can't keep up with our own pace.

We forge ahead at breakneck speed, fueled by the perception that we are running out of time. That perception, along with the cultural acceptance that busyness implies importance and value, drives us to exceed any reasonable list of daily to-dos. We can't remember what we're supposed to be doing, or what we've already done, without a download or an update because we're so distracted when we're doing-what-we're-doing. Our preoccupied mind-set lets busyness settle into our lives like an overbearing backseat driver; it's always a little bit out of view, but you know it's there because it never stops directing what you do, even though you're (in theory, anyway) in the driver's seat.

> *Slowing your pace can unclutter your thinking, boost your energy, revive your spirit, and awaken your passions.*

• Busy and Relationships •

As mentioned above, our behavior ripples out. As parents, we are teaching our children how to be busy. We feel that by overscheduling them, setting high standards, and providing them with the newest technology we are helping them *get ahead of the pack* and ready for a nitty-gritty, competitive world. And although we may be well-intentioned, our continuous quest to get more done in less time, and our efforts to teach our children to do the same, ends up incubating us from one another.

When busy pushes its way into our significant relationships, little room is left for intimacy. Emotional intimacy occurs when we allow ourselves to be present, vulnerable, and aware of our needs *and* the needs of our partners. When we are distracted by our pursuits, shifting our priorities so that our significant relationships fall in line behind those pursuits, we become disconnected from our partners. It's unlikely that we will be raised up and invigorated by our relationships if we feel tired, stressed, or unsupported, and it's doubtful that our partners will feel inspired to support us if they don't feel they are a priority.

In our professional lives, it might seem counter-intuitive that doing less and connecting more could be an effective formula for success. Yet when organizations value the importance of professional interpersonal relationships, they experience long-term benefits, such as better employee health, fewer absences, and decreased worry and anxiety. Cultivating relationships takes time and effort, and unfortunately, when doing so is not considered an important part of an organization's tenet, opportunities are missed and personal health and well-being are sacrificed. Imagine if we all slowed down enough to get to know the other people we are spending 50 percent of our waking hours with? Building professional relationships doesn't need to involve inviting our coworkers to dinner. We just need to slow down, be present, and get to know another person. Doing so builds camaraderie and communication and mutually focuses efforts.

• *What's the Price of Your Pace?* •

What's the price of your pace? Your health? Your relationships? Your career?

Now that you've determined the signs that it's time

for you to break up with busy, you can begin to advance that awareness and discover what motivates your busyness and the importance it represents in your life. The three questions below will help you begin your exploration of both.

1. What motivates you to continue your busy pace?
2. What value does your busy pace provide you?
3. What do you want, and what do you need, to make it happen?

Take a few minutes for each question and consider each with thoughtful consideration; it's a significant step that will help you gain clarity around your motivations so that you can begin your break from busy. These questions may not be easy to answer. Perhaps you've never thought about what motivates you or considered the concept that busy is a choice, a culture, a behavior, one that entices you to feel important and valued. Just by exploring these questions, you've expanded your awareness, and awareness allows you to recognize your blind spots and build on your strengths. So, congratulations! You're on your way to breaking up with busy and starting to live your life instead of just running the race. Understanding exactly what strategies you have in place that are keeping you busy and overscheduled is your next step.

CHAPTER THREE

Giving Busy the Boot
Kicking Your Busy Habits

The busy habit is just like any other habit — breaking it takes practice. You may be accustomed to rushing from place to place, saying yes when you really need and want to say no, or being the go-to person all the time, and it's exhausting! I'm sure you know far too well what that feels like and are ready to change for good. Merely scratching the surface of a habit provides only temporary feel-good solutions.

As we learned in the last chapter, you've got to dig down to get at the root of what motivates you and the value you derive from the habit. Motivation is the bridge between desire and action, and to make change stick, especially when changing deeply ingrained habits, it is your motivation that helps you remain focused on your goals, even when setbacks occur. Your motivation determines how likely you will be to accomplish your intended outcome. Knowing what value you've attached to that outcome is key in formulating your decisions associated with achieving your goals. Motivation aligns your efforts with your goals, and the value you place on that goal greatly influences your success in meeting it.

The next step is to understand how your motivations and the value of a habit play significant roles in your thought processes when setting up your strategies. As you shift your thinking, alter your timeworn habits, and discover your need/want connection, you can begin building new strategies that will help you kick your busy habits and make your life a lot more joyful.

• How and Why We Do What We Do •

We formulate strategies throughout our lives. These strategies are a set of tools we use to navigate our experiences, and they are significantly influenced by our parents or primary caregivers. As we grow and change, our tools evolve, enabling us to hone the ones that work well. We also may use ones that are not as useful or helpful, but we use them simply because they are familiar to us. Our experiences, the development of our strategies, and the evolution of these tools function as a script we continually refer to as we move forward. Values, morals, and societal norms influence our experiences and become part of the development and structure of our strategies. And as we have these experiences and employ these strategies, what emerges are habits. It's how we do what we do.

Charlene's story below illustrates how some people are really good at adapting their strategies and modifying their behaviors. Their ability to self-evaluate, shift perspective, and change an approach gives them a greater capacity to reinvent themselves.

CHARLENE'S OSW STORY

I moved around a lot as a kid. I went to six different middle schools and three high schools. Each time I had to find a way to make friends and fit in, and because I moved so much, getting along with people and making friends without getting too attached became a natural way of fitting in wherever I went. It also helped me advance in my career because I was able to build relationships without getting overly involved, and that worked for what I wanted to achieve. I learned to separate the relationship from what I needed to do. Where I struggled was in my personal relationships. It took me until I was in my late thirties to figure out what piece of that strategy wasn't working for me. My ability to distance myself was blocking me from true emotional intimacy. Realizing this was like having a light go on in my head — how could I have missed that piece? Well, I never had to use that before to get what I wanted, so I had to figure out how to adjust my strategy to get what I needed.

The good news is that we all have the capacity to adapt and the power to reinvent ourselves. As you make small edits to your busy habits, you'll begin building the bridge from where you are now to where you want to be.

Habits are strategies on autopilot. They are often our fallback reactions when we are stressed and busy. A habit consists of three primary elements: the cue, the behavior, and the reward. For example, it's 5:00 PM (cue), you pour a glass of wine (behavior), and you sit down and unwind (reward). Or your phone rings and you see it's your best friend (cue), so you answer (behavior). You know she always makes you laugh and you always enjoy talking with her (reward). The cue, behavior, and reward are the fundamental mechanisms that prompt automatic thinking, feelings, and actions. In simple terms, habits are the result of training. By repeating a certain behavior, we train our body and mind to perform it with less conscious thought. The more we access the training, the easier it is to form, implement, and maintain the habit. And the more we perceive the reward in positive terms, the more likely we are to use the associated training because it provides an outcome we want or at least one that we are familiar with. I got to learn this early when at age nineteen I was hired as a flight attendant.

Emergency and safety drills were a primary part of my training. Over and over the other trainees and I were put in potential disastrous situations, many of them taking place on a life-size simulator of an airplane's interior, such as crash landings with fire-like effects in a smoke-filled cabin with jammed emergency slides and blocked exits, and much more.

Part of our training was in a technique that would end up being a key method I would use in many other aspects of my life. It is called the Thirty-Second Review and takes place during the first three minutes and the last eight minutes of any flight, the times considered the most critical for flight emergencies. Seated on our flight attendant jump seats, we mentally ran through all the major emergency scenarios that might occur during takeoff and landing. This process works on the premise that whatever is in the forefront of your mind, gleaned from your training, will help you react, even when chaos and danger ensue. Some forty years later, as a passenger, I still do the Thirty-Second Review every time I'm on a flight.

Every day we use similar techniques to reinforce our habits to get what we need and want. For example, in meditation, I use conscious thinking to attune my thoughts to what I need (mental and physical recharging), and that is central to what I want (clarity, creativity, calm, and spiritual connection). I go to the gym every day not because I like to work out but because it's another way for me to recharge, stay relaxed, and enhance my health. Both habits are implemented often, both have positive rewards, and both advance my personal goals for living a healthy lifestyle. I'm motivated by the rewards I reap, and the high value derived from the outcome of these habits helps me sustain both as long-term strategies to get what I want.

Habits are familiar, which means we don't consciously think about how to use them. That's why adopting new ones, such as beginning an exercise program, feels more difficult and tiring. They take more thought. They take practice. After a while, new habits become easier to access, with less effort and more predictable results. The familiarity of a habit often blinds us to the fact that it is not healthy. That's why bad habits often undermine our desires to implement good ones. The key is to build new, resourceful habits that you can fall back on. The clearer you are about which strategies work for you and are in alignment with your need/want connection (which we will discuss further below), the more likely you are to automatically adopt those habits instead of falling back into your old busy habits.

> *Needs first, wants second; once that equation is in place, you'll be more likely to fulfill your goals and desires.*

• Is Busyness Keeping You from What You Need and Want? •

Certain strategies and approaches generally work well for shorter-term goals, the things we want to accomplish in the near future, such as taking a vacation, purchasing a new car, or paying off a credit card. Lifestyle changes — like breaking your busy habits — require a longer-lasting approach that develops into maintainable strategies and eventually new habits.

Changing your relationship with busy necessitates determining your need/want connection and how it relates to your goals. It's a cause-and-effect formula that when balanced will lead to more sustainable outcomes. For example, if you decide you want to lose five pounds in a week, it can be done. No problem. There are numerous people to tell you how to do it. But is that helpful?

Can you get the weight off? Absolutely. However, it's unlikely that approach will be sustainable in the long run.

When a client comes to me because she wants to lose weight and has tried several times, without success, to keep it off, I need to help her find the *why now* part of her need/want connection. If her motivation is that she wants to look better, or that she's tired of the extra pounds, that is typically a sign that she has not dug deep enough to make her goal sustainable. Her reasons just scratch the surface of what she really wants.

The broader the reason, the less likely the root of the *why now* has been uncovered. In this case, if she doesn't believe she deserves to feel or look better, her weight loss is apt to be temporary. How can she be truly successful until she knows the value of what she needs and how it will support what she wants? When she establishes both, her *why now* will be evident, and she'll realize her endeavors with less effort and more satisfaction.

Before moving on, let's explore your need/want connection. This is to help you develop the habit of considering your *need* first, before anything else. Think of it this way. If you know you want to change jobs, what do you need to make that happen? You may need to write a new résumé, network with business associates, buy a new interviewing outfit, and rearrange your schedule so you have time to search for that new job. You know you want a new job, and organizing your strategy for what you need to do first will put the ball in motion to make that new job a reality instead of merely a desire. Often we get so focused on what we want, we overlook what we need to think and do to make it happen. I'm asking you to take a close look at what you need so that your strategies are well formed and more likely to lead to your wanted outcome.

EXERCISE: The Need/Want Connection

This would be a good time to begin a Breaking Up with Busy journal. As you work through the exercises in this book, your journal or notebook can provide you with a personal map of each step you take to free yourself from the madness of busyness. It will also provide you with a rewarding feeling of accomplishment, which will encourage you to continue.

1. What do I really want?
2. What will change for me when I have what I want?
3. What do I need that will move me toward what I *really* want?
4. *Why now?* State your answer in the positive.

   I need _____ to
   obtain (what I want) _____.
   Why now? Because _____ meets my
   need and _____ is what I want.

When I first used this exercise, I was struck by how often my clients would list all the things they wanted before realizing they had said nothing about what they needed. When they did acknowledge what they needed, it was often a list of things, or what other people had to do first before they could do what they needed. Be mindful of that scenario. Consider your personal attributes and your strengths, and how you can apply them to secure what you need and then move on to devising the bigger picture for yourself. Being clear about all three will help motivate you into action.

• *Motivating Yourself out of Busy and into Action* •

Some of us take action to reach a rewarding goal, while others take action to avoid discomfort. Most of us are motivated by the first and temporarily eased by the second. When we cultivate strategies that are derived from well-formed habits, and our actions are supported by self-awareness and clear motivations, we set ourselves up for achievement. Understanding how your brain works when forming habits is a great tool for motivating yourself out of busy and into action.

The brain is a powerful, dynamic, ever-evolving tool that is always available, capable of generating an infinite range of subtle and vast changes. Each of us operates from our unique programming — how we interpret our world and how we communicate it to ourselves and others based on our experiences. In a blink of the eye we pull those experiences to the forefront of our minds, apply meaning, and express that meaning with words and behavior. And the more we do this, the easier it is to implement the strategies — behavior and thinking — associated with those experiences. This is where training meets up with habit. Simply by changing how we think about something, we can rewire our brains' response. When we're stressed and busy, our brains don't think clearly, and that's when we are most likely to fall back on our habits. That's valuable, especially for those with jobs such as first responders where habits — training — can be lifesaving. However, when we employ habits, which may seem useful in the moment but might not support our bigger picture, it's time to revamp those habits and establish new ones that work best for what we need and want.

Every thought we have is an ingredient of our personal reality. Our thoughts quietly direct our actions. For example, if you spend a disproportional amount of time thinking about an ex-lover, it's unlikely that you'll get over him or create any mental and spiritual space for a new person to enter your life. The same is true if you tend to focus on the problem rather than the solution; the problem will remain alive and well, while the solution will be given no space to grow. Your thoughts generate boundless possibilities for your life strategies, for how you manage your unique world, and for the expansion of your mental, physical, and spiritual course.

Your brain needs to be recharged, just like your body. Overworking it without giving it a rest has a direct impact on your overall health. Reprogramming your thinking wakes up your awareness and gives you a refreshed way of looking at situations and challenges. It's a reboot of cerebral assets. When we rest and recharge our thoughts — our brains — we can begin developing new strategies for mindfully choosing how to spend our time.

• *Your Life Strategies Review* •

Now that you understand the connection between your life strategies and how they influence and form your habits, you have assimilated the essential tools to shift, edit, or change both. And, having learned how to pinpoint your need/want connection, you are well on your way to breaking your busy habits and freeing yourself from your overscheduled days.

The Life Strategy Account Review will help you identify what's working for you and what's not. As you take account of each tool and realign your priorities, you'll begin editing your out-of-date strategies and designing your unique solutions for breaking your busy habits.

This review is a thinking reboot. It will help you access more mindful options for getting out of your busy habits so you'll feel more energized and optimistic about changing the habits that are holding you back. Either way, just by reviewing the questions, you have already shifted your awareness, and that is certain to drive you toward what you want.

EXERCISE: Life Strategy Account Review

1. What resourceful strategies are working for you? These are the strategies that incorporate your natural attributes and allow you to easily maneuver and manage your time, relationships, and personal interests.

   I use _____ strategy. This strategy uses my _____ attributes. I know it works well for me because I feel _____ during and after I employ this strategy.

2. If you were to let go of one unresourceful strategy, what would it be? How would letting go of it enhance your day?

   It's not working for me when I _____. I would/will let go of my _____ habit when I employ this strategy. I know doing so will give me more time to _____, and I will move closer to feeling/experiencing _____.

Take a few moments to reflect on the strategies you use in your daily life: Which ones bring personal pleasure, a sense of accomplishment, a joyful heart, and fulfillment not reliant on anyone else? Which strategies enhance your days? Which strategies time-strap your days?

Now that you know what strategies and habits are working for you, and you understand your need/want connection, you have the essential tools to begin giving busy the boot! You know what motivates you and what's important to you, and busy no longer needs to be a part of either. You know how to clear your mental space enough to see your way out of the busy culture. Now it's time to discover the best solutions for getting out of your busy traps.

CHAPTER FOUR

Breaking Free from OSW Traps

In this chapter you will be peeling back more layers of your busy behavior. You'll discover what trap is holding you back and how to plan your exit. You'll learn about the four traps women typically fall into, which I call OSW traps, and discover that they are built on two prevalent OSW characteristics (being well intentioned and overdelivering), on the *should*s and expectations of our busy culture, and on the repetition of familiar habits. Getting out of your traps is an honest self-exploration that requires a frank acknowledgment that what you're doing is not working, a committed effort to change what you're doing, and implementing the solutions listed for each trap. Your view is about to drastically improve as you rise above and out of your trap. Your escape ladder has arrived! Knowing which trap keeps you captive is the first step toward the exit.

> We fall into traps when we inadvertently attach our emotions to an outcome and allow those emotions to dictate our decisions.

• What Is an OSW Trap? •

OSW traps are like murky quagmires: you don't know they're there until you step in and begin to sink. Clients often describe their OSW traps as feeling stuck, frustrated, and often embarrassed that they keep doing the same things that cause them to feel that way. They minimize how they feel: "It could be worse." Or they feel guilty: "I really don't have anything to complain about." And quite often, perhaps to avoid the fear of uncertainty, they overgeneralize and make broad conclusions, such as: "This never happens to anyone but me." We likely fall into our traps because we take it as a given that we should do more, and do it better.

Traps are reinforced by the *should*s of life: I should be this person, I should do this, I should be like that. Self-judgment leads to feeling stuck, squelching our innovation and our creative problem-solving. We lose focus, it becomes difficult to find new solutions, and ideas become stagnant. When we stay stuck for too long, we run through each day with a gloomy uneasiness and cultivate the idea that nothing is ever going to change, and then we start making choices based on that belief. Then we feel even more trapped. The familiar habits, the *should*s, the judging and cajoling and the feeling of stuck lay just below the surface of our traps, like quicksand under grass.

Dominique's OSW Story

Dominique was working two jobs and raising two daughters. She was proud of her accomplishments, and as the first woman in her family to graduate from college, she worked hard to achieve her marketing manager's position. She had a second job to help put her daughters through college. Education was a value she instilled in them at an early age, and she was focused on ensuring that they both had the opportunities that she had persevered to make happen. When she began experiencing acute insomnia, she counteracted it by having a couple of glasses of wine before going to bed. When she grew drowsy at work in the afternoon, she reached for the candy jar at the front desk. Her schedule was so jam-packed that she cut back on her workouts, eventually giving them up altogether. By the time her girls graduated from college, she had gained more than thirty pounds. After her girls moved out, her empty nest abruptly hit her. Dominique slowly slumped into feeling apathetic about everything. She felt like she should be happier, more grateful, and that she should appreciate her newfound freedom. What did she have to complain about, after all? Everything had turned out the way it should have, just as she had planned.

At our first meeting, it was apparent she was overwhelmed and disappointed by how she had let herself go. And even though she had less stress and fewer time constraints, she still felt trapped.

Dominique realized that she had unintentionally continued the same lifestyle, even though she no longer needed to; her old habits were not only unhealthy, they were out-of-date and needed to be discarded if she was going to move forward and reclaim her health and well-being, emotional freedom, and a lively enjoyment of her independent lifestyle. Once she became aware of this, she was unstoppable in carrying out her new goals. She rediscovered the tenacious and hard-working attributes that had allowed her to graduate from college and raise two daughters while working two jobs. Her new awareness helped her discover the piece of her efforts that was holding her back. Her attributes hadn't changed; she just never slowed down enough to shift them to help her manage her current life well. Establishing clear goals allowed her to get what she needed to improve her life. She lost weight and kept it off, and more important, she's happy with herself. She is proud that she didn't give up — "it's not in my nature"— and even prouder that she has shifted her life to reflect who she is, not what she thought she should be.

Dominique's story shows how easy it is to continue habits, even when they no longer support our goals. Although it had a negative impact on her wellness, Dominique continued working two jobs long after she needed to. That led to developing a secondary set of unresourceful habits (drinking wine at night and eating candy during the day), which undermined the positive ones that had worked in the past (exercising and eating healthy) and led to her weight gain and disappointment. Her familiarity with these habits gave her comfort, and although they were not helping her lead a healthy lifestyle, that comfort was emotionally satisfying in the moment. When she was finally clear about this emotional attachment and how it was affecting her behavior and ultimately her choices, she recognized what she needed to change to get what she wanted. Her goals (to feel better, lose weight, add hobbies and leisure time) started to align with her choices (working one job instead of two, exercising, eating better), which supported her preferred outcome (living each day more mindfully, with a balance between her obligations and personal enjoyments). Outcomes are the result of our objectives and goals, and when they are well formed and thoughtfully considered, we succeed in reaching them. That alignment was her strategy for breaking out of her trap.

To break out of your trap, consider your desired outcomes separate from your emotional investment in those outcomes. Spotlight your attributes that support the habits you are using to achieve your desired outcomes so that you can consciously engage them. Examine if your habits are working for you, or they are just familiar. You'll do this more as you expand your self-awareness and set mindful boundaries.

• *Traps and Their Solutions* •

Let's take a closer look at all the most common OSW traps that we fall into. As you explore each trap, remain mindful of being in your heart and letting yourself feel what stirs you. Try not to judge your responses, label your reasoning, or defend your position. Each solution helps you continue to build a bridge from where you are now to where you want to be. Each time you practice the solution exercises offered below, you'll get better at them, and eventually they will become your new habits.

The Being All Trap

The Allure. Praise confirms that you are liked and accepted. More is always better; it sets the comparison scale in your favor.

Setting the Trap. Central to this trap is a need for reassurance, affirmation, and the acknowledgment that you're valued and appreciated. You apply enormous pressure on yourself to be everything to everyone. Your self-esteem meter is set to a flurry of activities, affirmations, and commitments, providing armor against feelings of inadequacy. *Always getting it done* is often at the expense of your well-being, distracting you from discovering what you really need and want.

Breakout Solution. To get out of this trap, you must slow down enough to take a look at your needs and wants, without being tied to the approval of others. Ask yourself what intangibles are missing in your life that you are trying to fill with busyness. You may need to let go of any unrealistic standards that you have set, or establish reasonable boundaries to regain your emotional independence. Lightening up on yourself will take practice, and shifting your focus from being *all* to being yourself is a key element. Recognizing that you are good enough because of who you are, not solely because of what you do, is part of your escape from this trap.

Additionally, you need to be conscious of your over-connection with social media; otherwise it will rule your days in tiny sound bites. The endless updates of who's doing what, and where, serves as a relentless reminder of what you don't have, perpetuating the comparison game. Limiting these kinds of distractions is essential in your discovery of who you are as a woman and not as a *doer*. It's grueling to try to fit into a role when it is not anchored in your true self. Practicing self-compassion is a nourishing way to begin letting go of the perfectionism attached to *be-all* thinking.

EXERCISE: Self-Compassion

Practice this solution at least once a day for as long as you need. Let this new way of thinking bring you the confidence to know and accept your true self. In the process you will make positive, thoughtful, and assured decisions more often and in less time.

Discovery Questions

1. Do you accept that others are not perfect?
2. Do you lend a hand when someone is struggling?
3. Do you judge others if their best isn't your best?

4. Can you feel love for others when they are in emotional pain?

5. Are you tolerant of others when they fail?

Now turn those questions into *you* questions:

1. Do you accept your imperfections? *If not, will you?*

2. Do you allow others to help you when you are struggling? *If not, will you?*

3. Do you judge yourself and compare your accomplishments to others'? *If so, will you choose to stop or at least lighten up on yourself?*

4. Do you allow yourself to feel emotional pain and accept that this is part of life? *Will you acknowledge that you have been through pain and difficulty, and that most people you know also have, and that most, if not all, have survived, and even thrived?*

5. Do you allow yourself to fail, knowing that failure is part of trying? *If not, can you accept that failure opens you to learning more about yourself and that the only failure is found in not trying?*

Today, practice self-compassion!

- Choose one *you* question and turn it into action.

- Repeat the *you* action for five days, and then move on to the next.

- Once you have completed the list of five, revisit each as needed.

YOUR DAILY PRACTICE:
Nurturing a Mindfully Inspired State of Being

Practicing compassion begins within. When a situation or conversation arises that stirs feelings of inadequacy or perfectionism, pause your reaction and use one, or all, of the statements below to bring you back to a mindfully inspired state of being. Prepare by taking five deep breaths, and repeat one or all of these statements:

1. *I will give my imperfections space — they are a part of me.*
2. *I will allow others to help me. In doing so, I will be giving them the opportunity to experience the gift of giving, and me the gift of receiving.*
3. *I will allow myself to give my accomplishment mindset a day off. I'll be curious instead of doing things.*
4. *Whatever emotions show up today, I will stand back and observe them. I'm not a fixer today, I'm an observer.*
5. *Today, if failure shows up, I will choose to accept it as opportunity. I'll look for the silver lining and see it as a gift to me. I accept my whole being just as I am.*

Know that you don't have to be everything to be enough.

The Keeping Up Trap

The Allure. This trap provides reassurance that accumulating the right stuff will give you prestige and garner recognition from your reference group, people you identify with and who have similar attitudes and values. Their acceptance is the yardstick by which you measure your successes and self-worth.

Setting the Trap. This trap is built on comparisons: financial, personal, social, and professional. Driven by the desire to fit in, to be part of the group, we fall into this trap, which is a relentless measuring of what we ascertain to be important and necessary to be a part of the group. More is better, and better is more. The more, better, brighter, bigger, shinier obsession is a wobbly construction — a house of cards. Someone else's life may look better to us, but we can never really know what goes on behind closed doors. The reality of another's life might be entirely different from your impressions of it. The promise of having it all is pranced in front of us through a myriad of marketing channels. The chasm between the haves and the have-nots was only widened with the arrival of the internet. Online shopping erupted, and with it came the habit of purchasing the trappings of an upscale lifestyle at a fraction of the original price. This illusion of *fitting in* may shield us for a while but ultimately cannot quiet the anxiety we feel as we race to keep up. Consumption is, well, consuming, and the abyss that lies between what satisfies us and what we feel is necessary to move upward continues to widen.

Breakout Solution. Knowing and feeling that you are *enough* begins with stripping down, not keeping up. You'll need to deconstruct that facade to build your sense of self, without the trappings of consumption. Take a look at those who have all the external trappings of having "made it." Is this really what you want or need to be your true self? Dig down to find what motivates you to purchase, accumulate, and participate in this game of comparison. Focus on your attributes, and if you need reassurance or support, rely on your inner circle. These are the people who are worthy of your admiration, attention, and consideration. They will not ask you to keep up; they would rather that you just showed up as you are.

EXERCISE: No Comparison

Discovery Questions

1. Who do you admire?

   - Write down their names.
   - What do you admire about these individuals? Choose one or two attributes that jump out at you. Be specific.
   - How is what you admire important to you? Is it their lifestyle, physicality, intellect, possessions, or prestige?

2. What do their attributes do for them?

   - For example: Sue is intelligent and brave; she has used these attributes repeatedly to achieve professional success. Or Sarah is creative and humorous; people love to be around her, and she has a strong group of friends.

3. What do you admire about yourself?

   - Write down your attributes. Using labels, such as saying, "I'm a good mom," will only scratch the surface. Instead, think about the specific attributes that make you a good mom, such as tenderness, honesty, and dependability. *Example: I am confident and compassionate toward others, I trust easily, I have strong intuition, and I'm pragmatic.*

   - Why are these attributes important? What do these attributes provide you? How do they improve your life?

   - When are three different times when you've used these attributes? Write one or two sentences stating the situation, the attributes you engaged, and how you felt about the process and the outcome.

   - Put both lists side by side — yours and the person's you admire — and compare them.

   - Are your attributes the same as, or similar to, those that you admire? If they're the same, do you feel energized or depleted? If they're different, do you want your attributes to be more like the attributes you admire?

- Are you trying to impress the people you admire? Will impressing them add to your life? If so, what specifically will it add?
- Do you feel energized or exhausted by the comparing game?
- In one sentence, describe yourself using your top three to five attributes and how you use each. Make the sentence short and concise, and repeat it when you need a reminder that you need no comparisons to know exactly who you are.

The Saying Yes Trap

The Allure. Pleasing others rewards you with acceptance and is reinforced by their praise. This predictable outcome is reassuring and emotionally satisfying, prompting you to continue. You feel that the more you meet everyone's demands and requests, the more you will be liked and accepted.

Setting the Trap. Being overly agreeable assuages fears of not being loved or lovable, a condition that was likely set up in early childhood. When parents are domineering and micromanage their children's every decision, over time this strips away the child's confidence and ability to think independently. Love becomes a condition of obeying. Compliance and people-pleasing drives your choice to say yes, even when you don't want to do what you're agreeing to. Our culture frequently places women in the roles of nurturers and pleasers and has largely informed our compliance with the societal norm that saying yes is more acceptable than saying no. This dynamic often results in passive-aggressive behavior, guilt, resentment, and exhaustion.

Breakout Solution. Pleasing others, and disappointing them, is a normal part of any loving relationship. Reclaiming your days will require you to break the habit of routine yessing and to trust that you will still be accepted and loved even when others are disappointed. Most likely saying no will feel uncomfortable until you have a few positive experiences under your belt. As for those who give you a hard time, or push you to do things even when you've stated your boundaries, those relationships may warrant evaluation or a conversation in which you restate your boundaries. Delivering your message with firmness and compassion is essential. The key is to get comfortable with your ability to echo your healthy no. When you can comfortably choose no as a response with confidence, you are not just breaking a habit; you are taking a vital step toward valuing your health and restoring body, mind, and heart.

EXERCISE: The Healthy No

Knowing when and how to say no is as much about setting healthy boundaries as it is about your health; always saying yes is a busy pursuit that leaves little time for your emotional and spiritual well-being. This solution will help you get comfortable saying no, meaning no when you say it, and learning to accept no as part of making space for your yes when the time is right for you.

1. *Practice.* Get comfortable with saying no. It may feel foreign, even wrong, in the beginning. That's a normal part of learning anything new. The first time you rode a bike, did it feel natural? It probably didn't but eventually you did it with confidence and skill.

2. *See it to believe it.* Stand in front of your bathroom mirror and say no ten times. This builds your confidence and lowers your auditory barrier to hearing the word *no*.

3. *Pick your style.* Practice saying no and change your intonation to give it different meanings. Let these meanings sink in.

4. *Say it like you mean it!* Watch your face, particularly your eyes, as you say the word *no*. The eyes really are the windows to the soul, and if what you're saying matches your true desires, then

your message will be complete — verbally and visually — in its delivery. If we don't mean what we say, what we're saying can often be misinterpreted owing to the expressions on our faces. As you watch yourself say your healthy no, be aware that your face is also communicating your message, not just the words.

5. *Mindful checkpoint.* Choose something in the past that you wanted to say no to but didn't. Even though you can't go back and change anything, you can practice flexing your *no* muscles with a familiar situation. Revisit the situation in your mind and respond with your healthy no. How does it feel? What will you change going forward? Be specific so that you can easily apply that discovery to your next encounter.

6. *Be mindful of all of you.* Be aware of the feelings that stir inside you when you're saying yes or no. By making a mental note of your initial response, you'll allow yourself time to pause in your reaction. This gives you time to explore other options beyond saying yes or no, and sometimes that is all we need to turn a situation around and say what reflects our authentic selves.

The Overgiving Trap

The Allure. Overgiving is often motivated by our need to protect our vulnerabilities and maintain a sense of control in our personal ecosystem. A feel-good factor gives us a feeling of emotional security (*people respond favorably to me when I give, and that feels good*) and satisfies our hopes or expectations of being appreciated. You may feel morally obligated (*it's the right thing to do*), or perhaps your overgiving fulfills a set of ethical principles you use in measuring your value.

Setting the Trap. Being in the giver role provides comforting predictability for the future while soothing self-doubts in the moment. It's difficult for overgivers to receive help, gratitude, or attention from others; it stirs feelings of personal exposure, and that's not a safe feeling. Not fully attuned to the intent behind your habitual giving, you may often overlook the difference between making things better versus making yourself feel better, and you may end up giving from a place of need and attachment rather than from a place of lightness and pleasure. Overgiving becomes a knee-jerk decision. This kind of giving is conditional: *I'll give, but I'm expecting you to let me know how much you appreciate what I've done.* This may not even be a conscious thought. Overgivers often sacrifice their own needs to give to others and can end up feeling drained instead of emotionally fulfilled.

Breakout Solution. Givers need receivers to complete the equation. If you're always the giver, you're taking the giving experience away from another and an opportunity to trust the give and take of life. Habitually questioning the motives behind others' gestures of giving rather than allowing yourself to unconditionally accept them shifts your focus toward judgment. It is a limiting strategy for gaining emotional protection. Take some time to be honest with your reasons for overgiving. Are you appeasing feelings of insecurity? Are you uncomfortable with asking for help? Do you apologize and feel bad about yourself if you feel you haven't given enough or you haven't given more than others? Just saying, "I'm going to stop being the overgiver in this relationship, this project, or this situation" will not shift this habit; uncovering your real motivations for overgiving will. Give yourself a giving intermission so you can explore these motivations.

EXERCISE: A Giving Intermission

Discovery Statements

1. *Giving situation:* It is emotionally difficult and uncomfortable to receive from others. Possible reasons: *Giving creates more opportunities for being appreciated, liked, and accepted. This strategy helps you guard your emotions and regulate your daily environment.*

2. *Giving situation:* Giving often feels expected and burdensome, yet I do it anyway. Possible reasons: *You are coming from need rather than desire, and this makes the giving feel heavy and expected of you. The reward is often out of balance with your*

expectation of what you feel you should do or what you feel others should do.

3. *Giving situation:* I often bring a gift to gatherings or events, even though it's not expected. Possible reasons: *Giving reassures you that you'll be accepted into the group. Gift giving in these situations can lessen feelings of inadequacy or the fear of being judged. The gift functions as an emotional barrier against many of these feelings.*

4. *Giving situation:* It's difficult for me to ask for help, even from my close friends and family. Possible reasons: *Asking for help may prompt feelings of vulnerability. To maintain the persona you've created, and avoid being let down by someone not coming through for you, you often choose to do everything yourself.*

5. *Giving situation:* I give often because I want to please others. Possible reasons: *It makes you feel exceptional, loved, and admired. It means you are good enough and if you're good enough, you're safe.*

Overgiving Questions

Now that you have explored some of your motivations for overgiving, exploring the next set of questions will provide steps on the ladder for climbing out of this trap. The Overgiving Questions are a quick checklist for setting boundaries in the moment and an assessment for determining whether you are acting from your own desire or from habit.

1. Is this something I *want* to do, or is it something that I feel I *should* do?
2. When I think about doing this, do I feel filled up or drained?
3. What do I intend to get out of overgiving?
4. Would I ever be an anonymous giver?
5. Can I step aside and allow someone else to be in the giving position?
6. What feels uncomfortable when someone offers me help?

Now look at your answers and copy the essence of your answers into your Giving Intermission Statement:

I choose to give today because _____, and I will feel _____ after. This energizes me and fills my heart with _____ and my time with _____ _____.

Next time, before jumping into the overgiving role, ask yourself at least three of the above questions. Remember to respond to your feelings by pausing first instead of just reacting to them. This gives you time to explore your true intentions for giving.

Your life is happening now, and you're learning to slow it down so that you can be in charge of how it flows. Discovering your OSW type is the last piece in shifting your time-consuming busyness, being mindfully in charge of that flow and living to your fullest potential, as opposed to your fastest pace. Let's turn to that now.

CHAPTER FIVE

The Best Solutions for Your OSW Type

You have arrived at the threshold of change! You are now ready to identify your OSW type, which will help launch you out of your trap and into a new way of living. Each OSW type has specific mind-set practices and busy-busting solutions, which are the key tools you'll use to guide yourself, one step at a time, out of busy and into your mindfully designed life.

The mind-set practices are a vital part of your successful change process and provide the foundation for effective and propitious application of the busy-busting solutions. The mind-set practices are mindful exercises that positively boost your conscious thinking processes so you can better develop your mental plan before taking practical (verbal and physical) actions. This mental preparation allows you to more efficiently implement each of the busy-busting solutions and will powerfully support your busy-busting actions. All of the practices and solutions represent the fundamental tools for your vibrant transformation! Each is listed in its entirety in part 2, where we'll more fully delve into these tools, all designed to help you feel empowered to show up for others without giving away yourself. For now, let's explore the various OSW types, which will help you discern your own type as well as the best solutions for you.

• Getting Started •

This exploration is about finding a new path out of your OSW trap, not just setting a different one. Tuning in to your internal responses and connecting those responses with your external actions will help you expose the feelings that are most likely generating your busy choices. Here, I have laid out the tools for you to make that connection so you can begin living as the type of woman you define without the burden of busy.

Below you will find quick profiles of all the OSW types, which reflect the combined strategies, predominant characteristics, and conflicts that my clients and other women have shared with me. You can use one or all of the self-care tips, practices, and solutions provided when you're ready, on your schedule. Each is designed to facilitate your personal exploration and to help you discover and acknowledge your attributes, expose any unresourceful traits, accelerate your transformation, and reveal your best mind-set practices and busy-busting solutions.

The Pleaser: She Has a Heart of Gold

Traps: Saying Yes and Overgiving

Resourceful Characteristics

A Pleaser is one of the nicest people you know. She is always helpful, and in a crunch she's the one to call. Can't get to school on time to pick up the kids? Call her. Don't have anything to wear to that special event? She'll lend you her best outfit. She is the ace assistant who puts out the fires before you see an ember. She protects your schedule so you don't have to and always has things done ahead of time. She is always on time because she is dependable and prides herself on getting things done with a smile and a sunny attitude. And if there is an underdog, she's in her corner with praise and support.

Unresourceful Characteristics

She spends a lot of time doing things for other people and in the process finds it difficult to allow others to do things for her. Others seldom offer help because she is always so willing to be the helper. Her fear of "messing up" is likely to stem from early conditioning, usually from a parent who was emotionally unavailable, highly critical, and offered conditional affection. The Pleaser's mind-chatter sounds like, "If I don't please you or do it just right, you'll be upset with me and might leave me, ignore me, or chide me." This chatter is the subconscious root of her self-criticism and her preoccupation with what others think of her. She may have a tendency toward co-dependent relationships, passive-aggressive behavior, and personalizing others' comments or actions.

Self-Care

If you are a Pleaser, begin caring for yourself with the following practices:

- *Use your inner circle to practice saying no.* Let those in your circle know that you are developing better boundaries for yourself and that you would like their encouragement and support. You'll be amazed at how quickly they will jump in and lend you a hand — and you deserve it!
- *Explore your early experience.* Give yourself permission to let go of the past. Move forward and look ahead so that you can change your narrative to the one you desire and let go of the one that was.

Reset Your Mind-Set Practices

The Power of Your Beliefs (p. 102) * Astounding Change (p. 107) * Permission (p. 120) * Gratitude (p. 105) * I AM (p. 127)

Busy-Busting Solutions

Healthy No (p. 135) * Count Your Yessings (p. 143) * Rate the Rush (p. 155) * Mind Your Mantra (p. 151) * Setting Healthy Boundaries (p. 149) * The Artful Ask (p. 152)

The Time Optimist: She Has Time, Just Not Right Now

Traps: Being All and Keeping Up

Resourceful Characteristics

The Time Optimist always has many irons in the fire. She is the coordinator of events and people. Her dedication and attention to details are extensions of her creative thinking and innovative skills. The Time Optimist is spontaneous and rolls with the punches. When things go wrong, she remains flexible and able to think on her feet. She is motivated by her dedication to her standards for finalizing a project, and delivering beyond expectation, no matter what it takes.

Unresourceful Characteristics

The Time Optimist sets no boundaries on her time, and she often bites off more than she can chew. She over-promises because she really believes she can get it all done, she often cancels at the last minute, and she is typically one of the last to arrive at a function. Arriving late is her way of letting others know that her time is valuable, that she is in demand, and that she matters. Her distorted time management has her rushing everywhere, with her mind-chatter echoing, "There is time to do just one more thing before…" She fears being exposed or judged, and her need to prove she is capable and likable pushes her to be in constant motion. The Time Optimist is persistent in accomplishing her goals. She bounces between multitasking and delegating, neither of which produces the quality she feels her efforts should bring. Not surprisingly, she finds it difficult to relax and is often anxious about what needs to get done next.

Self-Care

If you are a Time Optimist, try these suggestions:

- Remind yourself that you are not what you do.
- Slow down and listen to your heart; that message is truly who you are.

Reset Your Mind-Set Practices

Time and Space Uncomplicated (p. 109) * Silence Is Golden (p. 112) * Your Magnificent Inner Power (p. 117) * Gratitude (p. 105) * Create Vibrant Moments (p. 125) * I AM (p. 127)

Busy-Busting Solutions

Healthy No (p. 135) * Taming Time (p. 138) * Rate the Rush (p. 155) * Mind Your Mantra (p. 151) * Turning Off (p. 157) * Setting Healthy Boundaries (p. 149)

The Perfectionist: She Makes Beautiful Things Happen

Traps: Keeping Up and Being All

Resourceful Characteristics

The Perfectionist is highly driven and accomplishes numerous goals. She has a methodical and detail-oriented approach and is exceedingly capable. Her look is flawless and effortless, her fashion sense spot-on. She is a consummate host and an artistically creative woman. She has exceptional taste in all things beautiful. The Perfectionist is dependable, prudent, and decisive. She is goal oriented and result focused. Her ability to see the big picture makes her the ideal candidate for coordinating team efforts and inspiring others to improve their performance.

Unresourceful Characteristics

If her perfectionistic tendencies dominate several significant areas of her life, they are likely rooted in fear of failure. This fear often leads to frustration, even depression, and can negatively impact her relationships and her ability to excel. The Perfectionist craves approval and praise and tries very hard not to disappoint her peers and loved ones. She has a strong need to maintain control in her world; it makes her feel safe. Her drive to excel and her mind-chatter, which sounds like, "Go big or go home," can derail her efforts if she loses focus of her big picture and falls into the swirl of her highly critical self-talk. She is her own worst enemy. Her fear of failure drives her workaholic tendencies. She struggles with vulnerability, since it heightens her fear of losing control. Feelings of inferiority can push her toward being judgmental, defensive, and overpersonalizing. She will often procrastinate to avoid doing something wrong or imperfect. Mistakes are considered intolerable.

Self-Care

Play it S.A.F.E.

*S*ay: Say what you need or desire. If you don't, you'll
    get more of the same.
*A*ct: Actions put words into motion. One mindful ac-
    tion each day can move you closer to what you
    truly desire.
*F*ace: Face your fear and walk through it. Acknowl-
    edging fear releases its charge and its power
    over you.
*E*volve: Saying what you want, putting it into action,
    and identifying your fear will allow you to evolve.

Reset Your Mind-Set Practices

Sparking Vulnerability (p. 123) * Permission (p. 120) *
I AM (p. 127) * Your Magnificent Inner Power (p. 117) *
Gratitude (p. 105)

Busy-Busting Solutions

Healthy No (p. 135) * Flip (p. 145) * Mind Your Mantra
(p. 151) * Rate the Rush (p. 155) * Take Five (p. 156) *
Turning Off (p. 157) * The Artful Ask (p. 152)

The Sorority Sister: One for All, and All for One!

Traps: Keeping Up and Overgiving

Resourceful Characteristics

The Sorority Sister places a high value on including
others. She can easily motivate a crowd and bring any
group together while making certain that everyone has a

memorable experience. Her civic-minded commitments include volunteering regularly and enthusiastically participating when asked or needed. She easily juggles her day with a lighthearted and carefree attitude. She is friendly, highly sociable, and in the know, and she wants the best for everyone. The Sorority Sister is loyal, resourceful, and an expert planner. She gets things done with a spirited approach. In her professional world, she is the one who can motivate the team, inspire others to excel, and build relationships that reach across the aisle. She is good at negotiating without losing her cool.

Unresourceful Characteristics

The Sorority Sister has a strong desire to belong. She self-identifies as a member of a group and is often unsure of who she is as an individual. Her need to be liked and accepted often motivates her to do things without a sincere purpose other than to influence the opinions of the group she wants to be a part of. Her self-confidence is dependent on the approval of others, and she feels insecure when approval is not forthcoming. She is uncomfortable with being alone, since it reaffirms her fear of not being good enough. Status is important to her, although she is the last to acknowledge that. Her mind-chatter is, "Make it happen," and she can become quite competitive in getting what she wants.

Self-Care

- *Build your self-confidence.* Take a few moments and jot down three attributes that you like about yourself, such as, "I'm patient and reliable, and I have an open heart."

• *Turn your attributes into an affirmation.* Repeat your affirmation while looking in the mirror, once in the morning and once in the evening. This simple exercise will begin a new energy flow, one that helps you focus on what you offer from within, not on what you are doing.

• *Reserve time for getting to know yourself.* Plan on doing one activity once a week that is just for you and does not include others. Being in nature is rejuvenating; take a walk, hike, or just sit and enjoy the scenery. Just ten minutes a week can create a shift, and planning the time for these power pauses allows you to get comfortable with being you and makes space for reflection and connection with self.

Reset Your Mind-Set Practices

The Power of Your Beliefs (p. 102) * Silence Is Golden (p. 112) * Astounding Change (p. 107) * Permission (p. 120) * Create Vibrant Moments (p. 125) * I AM (p. 127)

Busy-Busting Solutions

Healthy No (p. 135) * Setting Healthy Boundaries (p. 149) * Flip (p. 145) * Coding Your Calendar (p. 134) * Rate the Rush (p. 155) * Count Your Yessings (p. 143)

The Alpha: Stand Back — She's Got This

Traps: Being All and Overgiving

Resourceful Characteristics

The Alpha is a natural leader with a magnetic personality. She is strong-minded and easily commands a roomful of people with confidence, skillful assertiveness, and enthusiasm. She loves a challenge and is resilient and passionate about winning. Her accomplishments, and there are many, represent more than achievements; they express her purpose and self-defined values. Her communication style is straightforward yet empathetic. And even though she is highly motivated and career oriented, she is compassionate and supports the individual efforts of team members. Her mind-chatter is, "That's not my problem" or "I've got this." She approaches her ambitions with a positive attitude and does not personalize others' opinions of her if they are negative. She is confident about her character and can easily detach her emotions from conflict. Many Alphas are loners and have no problem self-motivating and setting goals.

Unresourceful Characteristics

The Alpha may have a subconscious fear of failing or being average, and this can drive her to be overly competitive, aggressive, and domineering. Her discomfort in trusting the outside world sets the stage for her need to control her primary environment. Parental encouragement may have been constant and overindulgent, making rejection and failure rare. The Alpha can be manipulative, controlling, rigid, and condescending if her fears remain unchecked. She can be highly self-critical and may come off as aloof and uncaring if pushed toward her fears. Expressing vulnerability is difficult and often rouses feelings of not being protected or safe. Her overconfidence can interfere with her ability to be present, and she frequently misses social cues that can provide opportunities to connect with others and expand her circle of meaningful relationships.

Self-Care

- *Lighten up.* Take small steps toward allowing yourself to be vulnerable. Choose one situation in which you are not the decision maker. It can be as simple and harmless as deciding where to go for lunch or being the last one to choose your seat at the table. Let someone else have the floor; by doing so, you will soften some of your hard edges, making it easier and more desirable for others to get to know you.

- *Go with the flow.* It's not always your agenda. Be an audience for someone else. Let yourself experience the feeling of not performing and not deciding, and just listen. Let someone else take the lead while you shine the light on her.

- *Is it important?* Ask yourself why it's important to always be the one making the plans or setting the rules. Choose to let go of being the planner or rule setter once a week, and see how that feels. Choose something that is less important and observe how the person taking the lead responds. It's a good practice in finding a balanced flow of give and take.

• *Give your whole self a time-out.* This will give you perspective on what truly matters to you. Choose one day a week during which you spend ten to thirty minutes just *being*. This could be taking a walk without your cell phone or spending ten minutes of quiet time in your office or home. Quiet is to your mind as food is to your body; neither your mind nor your body will perform well on supercharged schedules and caffeine forever.

Reset Your Mind-Set Practices

Create Vibrant Moments (p. 125) * Permission (p. 120) * Time and Space Uncomplicated (p. 109) * The Power of Your Beliefs (p. 102) * Sparking Vulnerability (p. 123) * Your Magnificent Inner Power (p. 117) * Gratitude (p. 105) * I AM (p. 127)

Busy-Busting Solutions

Coding Your Calendar (p. 134) * Rate the Rush (p. 155) * Mind Your Mantra (p. 151) * Turning Off (p. 157) * Take Five (p. 156) * Taming Time (p. 138)

• *You Did It!* •

You now know the key components that are driving your overscheduled lifestyle and how busyness has become a culture, and for many, an addictive habit. You've learned what motivates your busyness, the traps that can lead to being stuck, and your OSW type. All that's left to do is to use the solutions that are designed specifically for your OSW type so that you can break up with busy for good!

Your Reset Your Mind-Set Practices and Busy-Busting Solutions are in your solutions toolbox, and next we will add your daily Super Solutions Process and Meditation Magic — all will help you increase your self-awareness while you make practical and mindful improvements to each day. You can now stop sprinting through life and start reaping the enjoyment that comes from slowing down. Set your own pace, and encourage other women to do the same. Reclaim leisure time without feeling like you are less for doing less. It's your life, and you get to decide who you'll be.

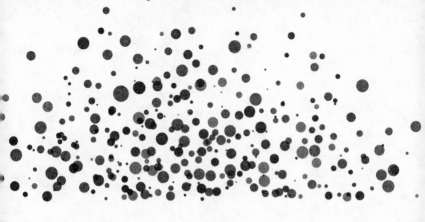

PART TWO

Solutions

TOOLBOX

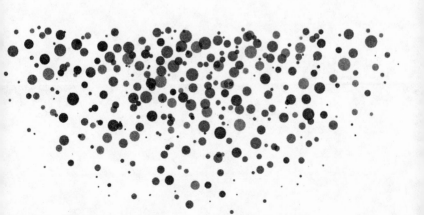

CHAPTER SIX

The Essentials

Now that you've explored your OSW type, it's time to put your specific practices and solutions into action. The Super Solutions Process and Meditation Magic are the essential tools that will help you turn those practices and solutions into agents of lasting change. By using them you will improve your skills of communication, negotiation, and collaboration. They are the cornerstone principles that put the *super* into your superpower!

• *The Super Solutions Process* •

The Superwoman in you is about to discover a new way to take off, and the Super Solutions Process is what powers that flight! This dynamic personal transformation tool will become your method for quickly assessing any situation and then redirecting your attention to the most beneficial solutions.

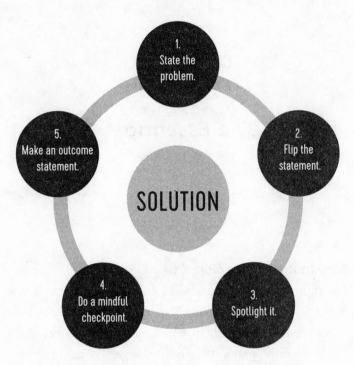

1. State the problem.

2. Flip the statement.

3. Spotlight it.

4. Do a mindful checkpoint.

5. Make an outcome statement.

SOLUTION

SUPER SOLUTIONS PROCESS

Solutions-based thinking and confident communication are at the center of this process, which incorporates three essential techniques: Direct Thinking, Whittling, and Sensing Meditation. Together these techniques help you jump-start your solution-based thinking, streamline goal-oriented actions, and draw your attention to both so that you stay on track to make mindful decisions. Let's take a look at the three techniques that make this process so effective:

Direct Thinking. Direct Thinking helps you verbalize your intention and mindfully direct your thoughts to support your actions. This technique galvanizes the power of subconscious and conscious thinking. Conscious thought uses more energy — brainpower — than subconscious thought. It is when we activate our conscious thinking that we can mindfully control and shift our thoughts. We use our conscious thought process when we are learning something new, making decisions, or solving a problem.

One of the ways your brain conserves its energy is by using the subconscious thought process. Our subconscious processes automate many of our basic daily functions and habits. Subconscious thinking is that autopilot thinking that gets us through the day and accounts for about 90 percent of what we think every day. When we direct our thinking using conscious thought, we can be more mindful and make decisions and choices that are aligned with what we want. Using our conscious thought processes can cultivate the right and most beneficial habits, strategies, and methods that will direct our subconscious thinking processes, and that's where we can mindfully affect our thoughts, feelings, and habits and take control of what we do and think.

Whittling. Whittling helps you distill your thoughts into a well-formed statement that conveys the essence of your preferred outcome. This technique edits out extraneous details, permitting you to focus on your action plan.

Sensing Meditation. The Sensing Meditation enlivens your five senses while you are in a conscious meditative state. You'll express your goals and their outcome by composing them as a story, as though they have already happened in real time. In essence, it's a meditative rehearsal of your future.

Before diving into the Super Solutions Process, let's first review just how vital your self-awareness is to the process. The more you uncover and connect with what is uniquely you, the more quickly you'll transform your thinking so that it is clear and decisive. Everything you need to make that happen is already available within you at this very moment. You are abundantly equipped to ignite your internal power to make the shifts that you desire. Acknowledging what you want, accepting responsibility that you make the difference in your life, and knowing that you can begin to do both at any time, is the kind of Direct Thinking that transforms solutions into vibrantly positive lifestyle habits.

> *The attention is on the solution, not on changing the problem.*

The practice guide below will show you how to implement your Super Solutions. With this process you will continue to disconnect from busy and to integrate a rewarding balance into your life. You'll experience magic each time you make this happen. Have fun with it!

Your Super Solutions Practice Guide

Your Steps at a Glance

1. *State the problem.* Make one quick statement.
2. *Flip the statement.* Turn the problem into a solution statement.
3. *Spotlight it.* Put your crystal-clear intention and attention on the solution.
4. *Do a mindful checkpoint.* This step combines spiritual awareness with the power of meditation, storytelling, and imagination.
5. *Make an outcome statement.* This is your personal declaration of what you have implemented.

> #### Power-Thinking Reminders
>
> • I want to change the pace, quality, and focus of my daily life.
> • I am responsible for making my life different.
> • I can begin taking one step at a time toward what I want right now.

State the Problem

Discovery Questions

Use the discovery questions to assist you in revealing what is under your statement — *the root* — so that you can move on to solutions and change.

1. What are you getting from the problem that feels familiar?
2. In one year, how will this problem look/feel to you?
3. In one year, how will this problem impact your happiness?
4. Do you want to stop living with this problem now?

Example

Problem statement: "I have no time to exercise because work takes everything I have."

1. What are you getting from the problem that feels familiar? *I'm really good at what I do; staying late is what it takes to stay on top and provide job security.*
2. In one year, how will this problem look/feel to you? *On the upside, I'll have demonstrated a good work ethic and excelled. On the downside, I'll probably have gained more weight and not spent enough time with my family, and I'll feel lousy about not making the adjustments I should or could.*
3. In one year, how will this problem impact your happiness? *I'll probably still feel frustrated and disappointed because I really want to feel more energetic and spend more quality time with my family.*
4. Do you want to stop living with this problem now? *Yes!*

The more attention you pay to the problem, the more energy and space it will occupy. The next step is to flip the problem statement to a solution and direct your energy toward your preferred outcome, not the distraction of the problem.

> *"Energy flows where attention goes."*
> *— Huna principles*

Flip the Statement

Your flip statement is a six- to ten-word solution expressing your ideal outcome. It's your mission statement — to the point and short enough to remember.

Discovery Questions

1. By making this change, what will you get that you don't have now?
2. What will change, and how will you know it's changed?
3. State your problem as a solution.
4. Whittle your solution statement down to six to ten words.
5. What is your flip statement?

Example

1. By making this change, what will you get that you don't have now? *When I exercise, I will have more*

energy, I'll feel better about myself, and I will lose a few pounds.

2. What will change? *I'll be more patient because exercise will help reduce my stress and anxiety. I will fit into my clothes better. And I will have more energy to do things that bring me daily pleasure.*

3. Problem statement: *I have no time to exercise because work takes everything I have.*

4. Whittling: (1) *I will leave work on time and give myself the time I need to exercise.* (2) *I will make thirty to forty-five minutes a day to work out.* (3) *My workout today is thirty minutes at 5:00 PM.*

5. Flip statement: *My workout today is thirty minutes at 5:00 PM.*

> You are the gatekeeper of your life. You set the limits, expectations, and possibilities.

● Spotlight It

Now that you've made a clear flip statement, you're ready to make it *crystal-clear* by spotlighting your intention and attention on the solution.

Stating your intention will make it more real to you. It will activate your hearing sense and bring your thoughts in line with your goal. This in turn will trigger your subconscious thinking to help you make choices that are directed toward that goal.

Focusing your attention will help you disengage from distractions that are undermining your goals. If it's not working for you, then it's not working. Distractions are flirty and enticing and often created subconsciously because we are trying to avoid things that we fear or are unsure of. Focus on changing that narrative so that your attention is on what you need and want, not on what you want to avoid. Use a mantra that will get you back to your intended frame of mind. Repeat the word until your attention is once again focused. My go-to mantra is "Honor thy thoughts." By using the word *honor*, I have put my attention on the priceless value my thoughts represent.

Your Spotlight Scenario

1. Flip statement: _____
   _____

2. My intention: State the purpose of your efforts.
   _____

3. My attention: State this in the positive. How is it connected to your goal? Be specific. What exactly are you focused on doing and thinking that will move you forward toward your goal? _____
   _____
   _____

4. My anticipated results will be: _____
   _____
   _____

Reinforce your Direct Thinking with the Direct Thinking Tools.

Do a Mindful Checkpoint

This step integrates your Direct Thinking technique with Sensing Meditation, combining attentive decision making with imaginative mindful storytelling and capturing the essence of your focused thoughts and actions. Your five senses vibrantly participate in this fun and lively meditation technique. Make the details as vivid as a page from a movie script.

MEDITATION: Three-Minute Sensing

Begin by putting yourself in your ideal outcome as though you were living it in real time. Use the following to bring it to life.

Set the Scene

Temperature: warm, cold, breezy, rainy, sunny, windy

Lighting: sunlight, moonlight, daylight, nighttime, natural, artificial

Sounds: environmental, natural, animals, people, music

Taste: flavor, texture

Smells: natural, perfumes, foods, people, surroundings

Act the Scene

Using the spotlight scenario you developed in the spotlighting step, meditatively act out your scene to its conclusion. Let yourself feel your emotions and sensations, and linger in that feel-good state. Develop a closing statement such as, *I'm focusing on the intention of my ideal outcome/goal in this moment.* This is another tool for keeping your goal present and conscious, especially when distractions attempt to pull you away. Repeat it often and with fearlessness.

Source Invitation

Consciously invite the power of your faith or spiritual connection to participate with your purposeful intentions and focused attention on the solutions: *I now invite the energy around me to participate in the solution/goal/outcome I desire. I trust that the strength of the Universe/Source will guide me in the direction I am meant to go.*

It is in the unexpected that we often find unforeseen opportunities to be whole and awakened.

Make an Outcome Statement

You're here! This is when the magic begins to happen; the evolution of your thoughts, the power of your purpose and focus, and your mindful awareness are merging, making your Super Solutions the structure of your daily solutions method. Answering the review questions below will help you construct your ideal Outcome Statement.

Discovery Questions

1. What will this outcome give me?
2. How will I know when I have it?
3. What is my ideal outcome (stated in the positive)?
4. Whittle your answer down to a six- to ten-word ideal Outcome Statement.

Example

1. What will this outcome give me? *Making time to meditate each morning will help me feel calmer and more capable of handling my stress, and it will give me time to replenish.*
2. How will I know when I have it? *I will know I have it when I feel a sense of calm and hopefulness. I will feel I have taken better care of myself by giving myself the time I need to reflect on what I truly want and to focus on optimistic solutions instead of my fears and worries.*
3. What is my ideal outcome? *I will be alert to what I need and want and have the confidence to make both happen. My positivity will increase, which will greatly influence my sense of playfulness and improve my emotional connections with my loved ones.*

4. Whittling: (1) *Meditation is time for me to focus on the positive aspects of my life. I have the confidence to explore and get what I need and want. My emotional connections will increase and be more fulfilling.* (2) *Meditation is my time to focus on the positivity of my life. I have the confidence to have what I need and want and to feel loving and strong connections with my spouse and children.*

5. Outcome Statement: *Meditation emphasizes the loving and positive connections in my life.*

Now you know exactly what you want. You have awakened and merged the power of your nonphysical and physical attributes to bring the most ideal outcome to you. Allow your attention to stay focused on the process and your five steps, not just on the outcome. Trust the process to unfold as it is meant to. And if it turns out to be different from what you expected, be open to what presents itself. It is in the unexpected that we often find unforeseen opportunities to be whole and awakened.

Keeping Your Super Solutions Powerful

For this process to work, you've got to put it into action. As you go forward, keep the following tips in mind:

- Work on one change at a time — focus on making it significant, not instant.
- Build your confidence and ability by practicing the process with minor situations or challenges.

- Keep your focus on the big picture. Don't get stuck in the details.
- When you experience uncomfortable feelings or uncertainty about your direction, go back and use the Super Solutions Process to remove what is blocking you.
- Practice the process often. Practice makes better, not perfect.
- Vulnerability is part of growing. Be bold, be brave, and kick butt!

> *Work on one change at a time — focus on making it significant, not instant.*

Direct Thinking Tools

- Repeat your intention to yourself at least five times daily.
- Write down your intention, and place it anywhere that you can easily revisit it throughout the day.
- Commit to upholding your intention.
- Pay attention to what is working, and repeat it.
- Step out of conversations that distract you from your mindful choices.
- Engage in activities with those who have similar goals that support your own.

- Pay attention to your thoughts, and recognize that they are in your control.
- Thoughts can be helpful or a hindrance — you make that choice.
- Your mind is a sacred place. Choose thoughts that honor that place.

By practicing and implementing the Super Solutions Process, you have elevated your solution-based thinking with practical methods and used your personal attributes and your abundantly present mindful energy to know what you need and how to get what you want.

• Meditation Magic •

Meditation is both practical and spiritual, and in my experience, it can be described as "magic." It's going to be one of the most important tools you'll incorporate as you break up with busy and find new space for what you want. This brief and effective method is like having an assistant in your pocket, one that will help you clear your *mental desk* so that you can focus on what you mindfully choose. You'll experience an improved state of being as you consciously state your intended desires for your day. It is a quick edit to help you revise, recalculate, or plan the best moments you can imagine.

Meditation improves many functions of the body such as lowering blood pressure and stimulating the region of the brain (prefrontal cortex) responsible for emotions and behavior. It is also a rich and infinite Source for connecting with your spirit and soul. Simply stated, the soul is the provenance of all living beings, the heart of humanity, the eternal and formless connection of each of us as one. The soul is imperishable and boundless, the consciousness of life as experienced by each of us as individual to self. Soul rises through spirit. Soul is one with self, and spirit is one consciousness held by all. Both are present in all we do, even if we are unaware of them.

Our thoughts are the only representation of consciousness that we can shift, manage, and change. Mindfully managing your thoughts through meditation can quell worry and anxiety, improve your sleep, improve concentration and self-awareness, boost your immune system, and help reduce the overall effects of stress. There are numerous types of meditations, and all will help settle your mind-chatter. Using rhythmic breathing, Meditation Magic focuses on consciously activating your thoughts and directing them toward a specific goal. It is a simple technique with lasting effects. And don't limit yourself to three minutes! It's likely that once you adopt this method it will become so rewarding and enjoyable, and profoundly powerful, you'll want to extend the time of your meditation practice. Start with three minutes and add more as you feel you need and want.

THREE-MINUTE MEDITATION MAGIC:
Calm and Clear Meditation

1. Find a comfortable, safe, and quiet place.
2. Sit tall and with honor, your feet flat on the floor, arms and palms relaxed at your sides.
3. Take five deep breaths: inhale through your nose and exhale through your mouth. Then let your breath relax and find its natural rhythm.
4. Imagine yourself releasing tension with each exhale and inhaling positive energy with each inhale.
5. Set your intention for your meditation: *I ask and intend for _____. I ask that a clear and sacred place be present, free from distractions that are not aligned with my intention.*
6. Take five deep inhales and exhales.
7. With your next set of five inhales and exhales, imagine a clear, warm, golden light floating just above the top of your head, and with each inhale bring the golden light into your body, beginning at the top of your head. As this light fills you, you will begin to feel your muscles and your mind and body start to relax. Continue to visualize this light as it gently and smoothly moves down and through your body until reaching the bottoms of your feet. Go as slowly as you need. As the light passes through the bottoms of your feet, you

will feel your reconnection with Mother Earth. You may feel a tingling warm sensation as your conscious energy passes through the bottoms of your feet and as you connect deeper with earth energy.

8. Set your focus for the day: *Today, I choose to focus on _____. I will be aware of _____. Today I choose to give _____. Today I choose to receive _____.*

9. Give thanks to your source of faith. Create your day in the light of your source of faith.

This is a quick and effective practice, and it's fun! Expect and trust that what you give and receive will be a part of your meaningful day.

The Super Solutions Process and the Meditation Magic are your dynamic duo for advancing breakthrough communication with anyone or in any situation and for advancing powerful restorative thinking methods. Use both essentials to revamp your negotiation skills and to cut the extraneous distractions that pull you away from your day and undermine your efforts to stay clear of busyness. They are incredibly effective techniques, easy to learn and implement, and will help you stay on track. The next chapter's mindful practices build off these tools, transforming your aspirations and ambitions into long-term accomplishments.

CHAPTER SEVEN

Reset Your Mind-Set
Mindful Practices
for Phenomenally Powerful Thinking

The purpose of this chapter is to bring to light the phenomenal power that the right mind-set can give you, as well as the methods for tapping into it, so that you can continue to create a solid foundation for conscious decision making and change. These are the practices that I suggested for each OSW type in chapter 5. Use the ones that fit your particular type or explore all of them; these real-life practices will continue your breakup with busy and enhance the quality of any day.

The right mind-set inspires, guides, and supports your decisions to successfully accomplish your goals. Your beliefs play a big role in this, influencing what you think and therefore what you do. When your mind-set is in harmony with your beliefs, your actions will be in harmony with both.

Think of your mind-set as a script and your actions as the movie. You've got to write the script before the movie can be made. It's got to tell a story that makes sense and that follows an order in how it unfolds. If the camera starts to roll before the actors have rehearsed the script, it's a mess and takes more time to get right. Resetting your mind-set is your rehearsal for doing what you want to do; it gets your thinking prepared so you're ready for action. The practices in this chapter will help you strip out the dispensable thoughts and mental habits that don't support your script; they will open up your thinking so that you have the right mind-set for astounding change.

• *Mindfulness Practices* •

These practices help you unwrap rote thinking that often gets in the way of discovering new solutions. Mindfulness is one of the best ways to train your mind to extinguish unresourceful thoughts so you can consciously direct them to solutions. The practices below will dramatically streamline that process. You will refine a new and empowered way of thinking. And as you continue to expand these skills, your transformation will breathe new life into your mind, body, and spirit. Don't waste any more time doing things without the power of thought in place.

The Power of Your Beliefs

Our beliefs are derived from our past experiences and define much of our personal reality and how we make sense of our world. Beliefs are the opinions we hold true. They form our values and become the standards by which we conduct our lives. Both affect our behaviors and attitudes. Our attitudes are how we express our beliefs and our values. Knowing which beliefs and values influence your thinking is a time-saving insight for clear and mindful decision making.

If you feel your beliefs are holding you back, updating them will allow you to see which ones you need and which ones you can toss. The following questions will help you make changes that reflect the beliefs you hold in highest regard and that are aligned with who you really are.

The Practice

1. Which of your beliefs are working for you?
2. Which of your beliefs are no longer working for you?
3. Which of your values do you deem most important?
4. How have your beliefs shifted in the past one to five years?
5. Has that shift been useful, or has it stalled you in reaching your goals?
6. Which of your values support your beliefs?
7. Are these the beliefs and values you access most often to support your goals?

Example of shifting beliefs: Mothers should be the primary caregivers versus *Mothers and fathers are equally important as primary caregivers. We have only one life on earth* versus

Reincarnation exists. Each person lives her own life versus *We are all connected.*

Example of beliefs: *The Universe exists, miracles are real, I'm in charge of my feelings, intuition is always right, I deserve to be happy, I believe in the law of attraction, taxes are too high, spiritual healing works.*

Example of core values: Honesty, education, appreciation, ethics, perseverance, respect, loyalty, affection, enthusiasm

You've now distinguished which top beliefs are working best to get you where you want to be. These are your power beliefs, and they work silently and continually as part of your decision-making process. Practicing the Three-Minute Meditation Magic will increase the effectiveness of your power beliefs. It will provide space for strengthening your mindful connection so that your power beliefs become more potent and invigorated. The practice of assessing your beliefs from time to time rather than acting from a place of familiarity and comfort can provide a vital tool for remaining open-minded and empathetic and accepting of your needs as well as the needs of others. Decisions are easier to make when your beliefs represent your real and genuine self. You'll feel more confident making decisions because you'll know that you are truly the author of each choice you make.

Gratitude

Gratitude is noticing the good things that are happening all around you. Some goodness is more obvious than others, such as that of a loved one, a delicious meal, or a beautiful sunset. Feeling gratitude when life is stormy can be difficult; it's during times of hardship that our gratitude is most tested. Seeing the silver lining during those times is easier when we focus on the power of our gratitude.

Considering gratitude as a practice rather than a mood may help you to see it as an effective tool for personal health and wellness. Practicing gratitude raises your happiness meter, lowers your blood pressure, enhances your immune system, aids restful sleep, reduces anxiety and depression, and helps you to be more resilient. Just think about how much time you'll save, and how much of your time will feel vibrantly improved, just by taking a few moments to be thankful for the good stuff.

When we are in a positive, grateful frame of mind, our physiology shifts, stimulating feel-good hormones and uplifting our spirits. When others feel upheld, noticed, and valued, they are inclined to positively engage. Gratitude is contagious! Spread it around and share it often. It will vastly enhance the quality of your day.

The Practice

You can do this quick exercise anytime and anywhere. It can be as short as one minute or as long as an hour or more. You'll feel light and refreshed and in a mood of gratitude when you're finished. You'll be more alert to the good stuff that's present right now.

1. Find a quiet and comfortable place to sit down.
2. Close your eyes, and take ten deep inhales and exhales.
3. Imagine you are standing in an open field filled with wildflowers of all colors. Take a moment to see them flowing in a light breeze.
4. Using your power of imagination, invite your loved ones into this magnificent field of flowers. You are surrounded by all their loving faces.
5. Take a moment to see each of them, and then one by one, tell them the nontangible gift that they have given you, such as their understanding, kindness, or a loving partnership.
6. When you're finished, tell each one that you love them.

Repeat this gratitude exercise with the tangible things in your life, such as your home and the comfort it provides you, your car and the ease it adds to your life, the water that always flows from your kitchen and bathroom faucets, the trees that shade you in the heat, the birds that chirp outside your window. No matter what is happening, there is always room for gratitude. When you keep this attitude alive and active, you reap the benefits every day.

Practice gratitude daily by inviting it in with just one minute of acknowledgment at the beginning of your day and at the end. You'll be grateful for the attitude shift and the refocused purpose this mindful practice will bring. It is hard to feel sorry for ourselves, down in the dumps, or even frustrated when we take a few minutes to feel gratitude for what we have in our lives rather than focusing on what we don't. Keep that in mind and practice gratitude often; you can never have too much.

Astounding Change

What makes you undeniably you? I would say your natural attributes, the gifts you are born with. Unlike skills, which are developed over time, your natural attributes are harnessed from within and expressed externally through your passion and sense of purpose. Mindfully engaging those attributes, your gifts, and tapping into their unique power can create astounding change in far less time and with less effort than you may have thought possible.

Attributes are like a best friend; they are always there, willing to step up and move you forward. The more you access them, the more supported you'll feel and the less fearful you'll be as you master new and unfamiliar experiences.

Discovering your innate and plentiful gifts will help you to consciously access them so you can actively apply them in any situation, a mindfully unbusy way to finding the best solutions.

The Practice

1. *Looking back.* Thinking back as far as possible, what are the moments or memories that fill you with pleasure and joy? Which of your attributes helped make these memories? What is the common thread running through your memory? For example: *I was communicative, independent, sincere, honest, competitive, perceptive, trustworthy.*

2. *Lost in time.* Make a list of the activities, endeavors, or projects, both professional and personal, that make you lose track of time. This is where you are in the flow and where your passion and purpose harmoniously exist and flourish.

3. *Love-Leap-Live List.* Your Love-Leap-Live List is your written collection of the places you will go, the people you will meet, the accomplishments you aspire to achieve, and the experiences and sensations you desire.

   • *Love:* Who are three people you love and three places or things you would love to experience?

   • *Leap:* What are three things you would like to take a leap of faith to accomplish?

   • *Live:* What are three intangible improvements or qualities you want to bring into your life?

   • Take a few minutes to acknowledge the gifts you will use to make your Love-Leap-Live List happen.

- Do any of the attributes on your Love-Leap-
  Live List match the ones you accessed in the
  Looking Back and Lost in Time questions in
  this exercise? Which ones? These are likely the
  attributes that are most powerful, most useful,
  and most present to you in any moment.

Mindfully let them work for you to make the love
in your life abundant, the courage to leap more present,
and your passion and purpose more vibrantly alive. Busy
can't tempt you when your attention is squarely on all
three.

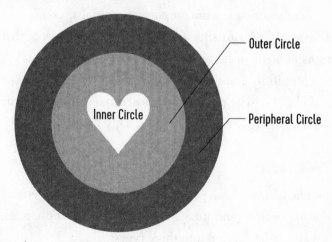

Time and Space Uncomplicated

TIME AND SPACE UNCOMPLICATED

Clutter-free living and the positive effects of feng shui
go beyond enhancing physical space; they also improve

our psychological and emotional well-being. When our senses are subdued and restrained by encumbrances and disorder, our minds become cluttered with distractions. We need space so that new opportunities for ingenuity, inspiration, and intuitive wellness can find us, and we need the time to grow more of each.

Simplifying your days is a matter of editing. It is removing physical items and opening mental space, bringing both together in a way that circulates the air around you, moves stagnate negative energy away, and attracts the kind of positivity that mirrors your dynamism. This practice is vital for shifting your reality to include a sense of ease and clarity.

Time and space uncomplicated, initially, consists of a series of adjustments, exclusions, and inclusions, that transmute into a calming habit.

Mindfully prioritizing your relationships with people and places will help you move closer to owning your time and managing the quality of your daily living.

The Practice

People. Choose how you spend your time by discerning the importance and quality of your relationship circles, which can be divided into three types:

- Your inner circle are your trusted confidants, friends, and family who are the most deserving of your time and space. They respect, accept, and expect healthy boundaries. These are your intimate emotional and physical relationships.

- Your outer circle are friends you see occasionally and your work associates.
- Your peripheral circle includes people you know incidentally and see primarily on special occasions. This group includes many people whom you don't know well.

Offer quality time to your inner circle first. Edit the amount of time and space you give away to each circle, and mindfully choose your commitments based on which circle that choice will enrich.

Places. Choose where you go and why you're going there. Ask yourself these questions:

- Is being there important to my big picture?
- Is it necessary for me to be there?
- How do I feel when deciding to be there?
- Do I want to be there?

Not everyone deserves the same amount of your time, and not every event or destination requires your presence; assessing these is a simple practice for determining their level of importance so that you can mindfully choose where and with whom you spend your time.

> *Nurture and share the content of your words — not how loud or how often you speak them.*

Silence Is Golden

Silence makes many people uncomfortable. We're generally conditioned to a fast-paced, crowded, and stimulating world. Silence is more intimate and heightens feelings of vulnerability. Think about sitting across from someone you just met, when suddenly the conversation goes quiet. Most people verbally fumble to get the conversation going or create a distraction such as excusing themselves from the table. The idea of silence is just not as acceptable as being heard, talkative, gregarious, or verbally charismatic. We tend to devalue silence as being less important and as not being the way to be strong players.

And yet silence is a powerful tool and is key in being an active listener. It's an innate skill that few take time to access, though it is available at any moment. The power of silence builds your confidence to be still, not as a doormat for others, but as an observer. When we assume the role of observer, we disconnect from emotionally charged feelings that can easily lure us into reacting rather than thoughtfully responding. When we don't have an emotional investment, we can let go of limiting thoughts and behaviors and be objective and empathetic. You can easily maintain your emotional center when using the strength of silence. Silence supports your capacity for mindful thinking, the kind of thinking that gets you where you want to go without the bluster of chaos or confusion.

The Practice

1. *Practice awareness.* Be quiet enough to listen.

    - Opening your awareness through silence can include meditation, quiet breathing, reflection, or active listening. All these practices hold significant power for change, growth, professional advancement, personal intimacy, and problem-solving. Active listening is perhaps the most untapped of the techniques. To actively listen, you must hold your thoughts and consciously direct them to be quiet. In a conversation, that means listening to what the other person is saying without judgment or formulating your defense or response. Taking the observer position in a conversation will help you stay in active listening mode and out of judgment and defense. To stay in the active listener position, keep these questions in mind: (1) Am I judging? (2) Am I preparing my response? (3) Can I repeat back the last three sentences spoken by my conversation partner?

    - The answers to the first two questions should be no, and the answer to the third should be yes. That's your formula for active listening. If you lose your listening center, repeat this quick phrase to get you back on track: *I'm a listener. I am here to receive these sounds as words.*

- Approach a conversation as you would if you were watching two people you had never met. They are having a conversation, and you are watching it.

2. *Be present.* Harness the runaway thoughts.

- Being present in the moment supports your active listening. It keeps your thoughts in the here and now, not in the past or future. If you hear yourself using words like *last time*, *again*, *before*, and *always*, that may be a signal that you are mind-surfing. Quieting your mind during active listening will stimulate your problem-solving ability, empathy, compassion, and the discovery of solutions. And it will dramatically reduce your response to stress and agitation. How can you feel stressed if you are simply listening?

- Taking one minute to set your intention before a conversation or encounter will vastly increase your ability to stay in active listening mode. If it's a conversation between you and an inner-circle person, agree to set your intention together. Doing so will support unity and help keep you on track during your exchange.

- Detach from your feelings, and be present to receiving the words of another. This doesn't mean she is right or wrong; it only means she has an opinion, a message, or some feelings that you are actively receiving through her words. Even when the situation is filled with emotion, stay aware of detaching from your feelings so that you are present. Your emotions are yours, not the product of someone else's actions or words.

3. *Observe.* Step back and take in.

- When you mind-surf outside your moment and gather up a big pile of past and future, your thinking and attention are elsewhere. To help yourself stay in the moment, focus on your breath. You don't have to speak or respond to be heard; silence is action. When you are the observer, silence *is* the experience, and you can be more open to listening. You can be the one who actually remembers what has been said or done by another because you weren't busy figuring out what you were about to say. When you remove your emotions from interactions and bring forth your silent observer, you'll discover details that are often missed by others.

4. *Let go.* Release your hold and move.

- When you let go of your expected outcome of a situation, you are letting go of your emotional attachment to that outcome. That's key in remaining objective, emotionally conscious, and powerfully effective. It allows you to receive the experience as an observer without the side-railing of your emotional attachment and investment leading your actions. Driving is a perfect example of how people let their circumstances dictate their emotions. In a traffic jam one person might welcome the opportunity to listen to a book on tape, while another might be boiling over in frustration. What's the difference between the two reactions? Both people are experiencing the same situation but are having a very different response. There will always be situations when our emotions lead our experience; however, pausing and taking a few moments to assess the connection between emotion and outcome may provide an opportunity to shift our emotions so that they are more in line with what we truly want.

• Letting go does not mean giving up; it means giving your awareness, presence, and observation to the here and now. All that any of us can mindfully regulate are our thoughts, feelings, and reactions. When you still your mind and quiet your thoughts, you'll be better able to confidently let go and trust the process of life, including the unexpected aspects. You'll recognize just how potent silence can be. Nurture and share the content of your words — not how loud or how often you speak them.

Your Magnificent Inner Power

Your imagination is your innate ability to be inventive and mindfully resourceful. When allied with conscious intention, imagination is a powerful daily tool and can be used to guide your thoughts into action and creative possibilities.

Imagination occurs across a vast mental space activated by a network of neurons in your brain. Artists constantly use their imagination, as do inventors, daydreamers, and problem-solvers. Yet our imagination begins to run amok when we spend time thinking about what we don't want rather than what we do. We encumber our minds with a plethora of mind-chatter and distractions when we worry about the *what-ifs* and the *maybes*. Our time spins away from us with thoughts of what someone did or said, or of what might happen or did happen, depleting our mental reservoirs. No wonder we're tired; we don't have any energy left to ignite our imagination and use this abundant resource that lays within us at this very moment.

Igniting your imagination will give you a sense of play, relaxation, and confidence and will help renew your focus. All are key in shifting ineffective thinking patterns. And making that shift will quietly and consciously begin to attract what you desire, since you are allowing your awareness to move toward those desires.

For some, using imagination is second nature. As children, we are frequently encouraged to use our imagination, but as we get older make-believe and imaginative play are often squelched and seen as frivolous. We lose the spontaneity that imagination offers in its inventiveness and infinite possibilities.

If you are out of practice, or if you're not convinced that igniting your imagination can really help, then I ask you to just try it, if for no other reason than to redirect your thoughts to something pleasant that has the power to recharge you at this very moment. Your imagination is a powerful tool for effecting change. Just think about all the amazing, innovative, and life-changing ideas and inventions that came from imagination; there would be no Disneyland, computers, or airplanes without it.

The Practice

You can spend anywhere from three minutes to half an hour doing this practice, which will help you ignite your imagination.

1. State your desired outcome, goal, or accomplishment in a clear sentence, using the following outline:

   - I will _____ (desired outcome, goal, accomplishment) in the next _____ (set your time frame for accomplishing your desired outcome).
   - I will feel _____ when I have accomplished _____ (avoid words like *good* or *fine*; be specific).

- I will know I have reached my goal because (state what will be different).

- Review your answers, and now add the details: dates, times, numbers, locations. Imagine that you are sharing your "story" with someone you don't know; providing details and emotions and telling the story clearly will deepen your connection with your goal.

2. Find a comfortable position to either sit or lie down in, your body relaxed.

3. Take three deep inhales through your nose, exhaling through your mouth.

4. Set your intention: *My intention is to disconnect from all distracting thoughts that are not aligned with my preferred outcome/goal. My intention is to focus on my desired outcome.*

5. Begin to act out your goal in your mind. Go through each step, each action, in detail. Paint the picture in your mind to give your story as much detail as possible: what you are wearing, who is there, the temperature of your surroundings, whether it is quiet or noisy, and what you are feeling. Walk your mind through each step slowly, and enjoy the process as though you are actually living this moment — because in reality you are.

6. Review your statement. Did you miss anything? Do you want to add any details? Ignite as much as possible — doing so is productive, and it's free!

Using this practice opens up unforeseen opportunities that would be left unnoticed in the hurry-burry of a busy day. Your imagination will never let you down when you consciously engage it as a positive transformational tool. Imagination provides us with a boundless canvas on which we can design our lives. So pull out your paintbrush, make your strokes broad and bold, or quiet and calm; make them your own, and ignite the inner power of your imagination.

> *If you wait for perfection to show up, you'll spend a lot of time waiting.*

Permission

What does it mean to give yourself permission? Maybe it's carving out enough time for you to reflect on the next steps you want to take in your career or a relationship. Or perhaps it means going on your dream vacation or taking a class in a subject you've always been fascinated in. Whatever it is, giving yourself permission to do anything begins with you, not with waiting for someone else to give you the go-ahead.

No matter what you feel is keeping you from granting yourself permission, fear is likely part of the picture.

Fear is a basic emotion and serves a useful purpose, such as activating our fight-or-flight response so we can move quickly in the face of a perceived threat. Fear is meant to be purposeful, not permanent. It gets big and abstract when we avoid acknowledging the source of it, letting it control us out of a vague sense of what it might be. When you reveal your limiting fear, you can then use it as an incentive to motivate you, not intimidate you. Everything you want is on the other side of fear. Once you move through your fear, new possibilities will likely be more apparent. And the timing doesn't need to be perfect; it just has to be good enough. If you wait for perfection to show up, you'll spend a lot of time waiting. Freeing your fear can be as simple as acknowledging it and saying goodbye!

The Practice

In this practice, you're granting yourself permission to go after what you want by first freeing your fear. Begin by stating what you feel is holding you back, and then use the following four steps to break that hold. Practice this process several times if needed; you will likely feel lighter and emotionally freer each time.

Complete this sentence:

I haven't done _____

because I feel _____.

I	2	3	4
Identify ➡	Hello ➡	Goodbye ➡	Resolution

1. *Identify your fear.* Exposing your fear will help you feel confident enough to conquer it.

   My fear is _____
   _____.

2. *Say "hello" and acknowledge your fear.* It might feel silly to say "hello" to your fear; in fact, it's even better if it does, since that silly feeling will help reduce the negative power of the fear. Accept the fear, and trust that you are fully capable of walking through that fear to the other side. You have to say hello before you can say goodbye.

   Hello, _____. I'm choosing to move through and beyond this fear to discover what opportunities and possibilities are on the other side.

3. *Say goodbye to your fear.* With your fear out in the open, it will be easier to say goodbye to it. Even though you may feel uneasy about saying goodbye, do it and trust that you have taken the first step in creating space for fearless emotions.

   I choose to say goodbye to this fear and to make room for more _____ in my life. Goodbye, _____!

4. *Permission granted.* Now that you have said goodbye to your fear, it is time to give yourself permission to bravely go after what you want. With fear out of the way, or at the very least out in the open instead of abstractly looming in your mind, you can address and move past it.

I give myself permission to _____

_____!

Affirm your permission by taking one minute every day to repeat it. Coordinating your thoughts with your verbal permission generates a stream of energy that will continue to move you in the right direction. To further strengthen this process, practice it in front of your mirror, add arm gestures to move the fear away from you, and wave good-bye to it. Bring it into the light, expose it, and release it.

Note: This technique is not meant to be a solution for phobias, terrors, or extreme psychological fears; those should be explored under the care of your medical advisors.

> *"Too many of us are not living our dreams because we are living our fears."*
> — Les Brown

Sparking Vulnerability

Embracing your sense of vulnerability can open the doors to new opportunities. Vulnerability is accepting intended, not dangerous, risk and taking a chance anyway. Vulnerability encourages us to face uncertainty and, even with no guarantees, to remain optimistic that meaningful purpose will prevail.

Practicing vulnerability encourages others to do the same, and in a relationship, practicing and sharing vulnerability fosters intimacy in all aspects. It's an essential act that will reap plentiful rewards — maybe not the first time but certainly more often than if you choose the familiar route.

If you do only what feels familiar, you will leave no room for exploring and growing. You'll repeat patterns over and over, zigging and zagging your way to the same results. It's okay not to know the answer, and in fact it can even be better when you don't — that means you're in the zone of possibilities, where innovative solutions and creativity can flourish.

This practice lets you get close to your vulnerability in a mindful way. "Un-ing" is a way to let go of certainty and to get comfortable with the unfamiliar so that when it shows up — and it will — you'll have the confidence to handle it without coming undone. Have fun with this — it's harmless, and it's easy!

The Practice

1. *"Un" your day.* Schedules and plans give us a daily framework to operate by — after all, we have a lot to get done. What would happen if you chose just one item on your agenda and undid it? Make yourself just a little bit uncomfortable by not knowing what will happen next. Not knowing is the basis of un-ing; in the unknown, possibilities appear and conscious thinking can be ignited. Your senses will light up to those possibilities, offering more creativity and clarity to your day. I'm always astonished at what shows up, things I had no idea I needed or that I would

enjoy, opportunities that have opened for me that I didn't even know existed. All are possible when we accept the uncertainty of the unknown and make space for it to show up.

2. *UNknown people.* Is there someone you've wanted to meet? Expand your friend circle, and extend an invitation to a new person to grab lunch. Be the initiator in a romantic interest. Invite a coworker out for an after-work drink. What's the worst thing that can happen? That he'd say no? That's okay. What's important is that you've put yourself out there to be vulnerable, in a safe way that allows you to grow.

3. *UNcheck the box.* Name three things that you do every day without thinking about them. These are things that if you didn't do them, your day would not be negatively affected; for example, making your bed, updating social media, shopping online, reading junk email, getting dressed (as in stay in your PJs), and being the peacemaker, motivator, or initiator. All these examples represent comfort zones. These daily *check-the-box* tasks and actions instill our sense of order. Today, choose one of these boxes to uncheck.

Create Vibrant Moments

Life can throw a lot at us, and if we're not mindfully prepared to handle it, and we let our reactions lead our decisions, we're likely to fall back into some old habits.

With daily stimulations and distractions, it's no wonder we struggle with being present.

Being present is staying in the moment emotionally and physically as much as possible. It is being mindfully aware of what is around you, hearing what is being said as though it's the first time, and applying conscious energy to assist you in doing so.

The benefits of being present and creating vibrant moments are many. Food tastes better because our senses are heightened, physical pain is lessened through mindful focus of breath and body, we can find solutions more readily when our thoughts are present and focused, and our gray matter becomes denser in areas of the brain responsible for learning and managing emotions. This mind-body practice also has positive effects on our immune systems, reduces symptoms of chronic stress, and increases our capacity for positive thinking. Talk about a time-saving habit! Being present extends beyond the moment; it allows you to create the type of day in which busy is just one of the moments, not the whole day. You'll calm your reactions to the unexpected and detach from the what-ifs. There's no time like the present to begin reaping the benefits!

The Practice

1. Stop what you're doing and envision a pause button in front of you, and hit it. This is your sixty-second pause, similar to the NLP technique that I experienced when I was asked to repeat my phone

number backward. It's just enough time to reset your mind-set and bring you back to the moment.

2. Breathe three breath cycles.

3. Keep your awareness on your breath: cool air in through your nose, and warm air out through your mouth.

4. Look around and mindfully imprint your physical presence in the space. This will slow your mind and bring you back to the moment. You'll begin to feel your energy shift as your thoughts move to a more conscious state.

   Example: *I'm in my living room, I'm standing, it's daytime, it's 2:00 PM, my name is Yvonne, I am a female, I am wearing black pants and a white buttoned blouse.* The more detail you offer, the more you'll increase your awareness of your immediate reality.

5. Now you're in the present moment. Begin creating vibrant moments whenever possible, and your better self will come to the fore.

> *"Don't let your past steal your present."*
> — *Cherríe L. Moraga*

I AM / Discovery

You've done a lot of work to bring yourself to this point. You've explored many questions and discovered how your mind-set influences what you think and do. This practice is an exploration of all you have acquired up to this point and is included as a practice for all OSW types, or for anyone interested in examining her capacity for personal growth and awareness.

Awareness is a lens through which we can explore the questions of who we are and what we want. Why does this matter? Because with expanded awareness you can question without judgment, have faith when uncertainty is present, love without conditions, and emerge from the confinement of labels and fully discover the I AM in you.

Who is the I AM under the doing, racing, rushing, responsibilities, and commitments? How can discovering your I AM release you from busy habits and overscheduled days and the guilt and frustrations that tag along with each? By knowing who you are, as defined by you and only you, you cultivate your capacity to adapt, evolve, and grow.

This self-inquiry reveals the potential of who you are right now. Nothing is set in stone, and there are no wrong or right answers. This practice was designed to help you discover yourself as I AM, not I DO.

The Practice

1. What does love feel and look like to you?
2. Where do you experience love most often?
3. What do you love about yourself?
4. Going back in time, what advice would you give

your younger self? What age did you pick, and what drew you to choose that point in your life?

5. Using your imagination and suspending all judgment, what do you really want? How will having it enhance your life?

6. What one action can you take today to bring what you want closer to reality?

7. What always makes you feel happy?

8. What have you discovered about yourself today?

9. What three words would you choose to describe yourself? (e.g., *eternal, ageless, explorer*)

10. What is your answer to the question, Who am I?

Sit with the answers to these questions for a day or so, or longer if needed. As you begin to contemplate the answers, be aware of what your heart is saying to you, not just what you are thinking. Remind yourself you are an explorer, curious about who you are and who you want to be. Once you feel you've answered the I AM question, use the Whittling technique in the Super Solutions Process to formulate your answer. Who you are is not what you do; what you do is because of who you are.

You've gained a better understanding of, and I hope, appreciation for who you are, an insight that will encourage you to be yourself more often, with authenticity and confidence. You understand the connection between beliefs, perceptions, and attitudes and how they influence your thoughts and behaviors. You're armed with methods that allow you to consciously shift from routine thinking to powerful and mindfully directed thoughts.

You've reset your mind-set, and now you're ready to tackle the solutions. Your thinking is in sync with what you need and want, so when you begin applying the solutions in the next chapter, your efforts will reap results faster than you ever could have imagined.

CHAPTER EIGHT

Busy-Busting Solutions

Coupled with your reset mind-set, your busy-busting solutions are designed to help you create a more stress-free lifestyle, enhance your ability to clearly communicate your decisions and desires, and reestablish your sovereignty over what you do and when you do it. In chapter 5 I matched specific solutions to each OSW type, and I note them here again. Work your OSW type solutions in the order outlined before moving on to the others. Doing so will expedite your final breakup from busy. The solutions that are not connected with your OSW type are a bonus and will further support your redesigned approach to how you think and what you do. Explore each one on its own, and at a time that works for you.

Each solution has a practical component that can be easily integrated into daily descheduling and time management. These tools will support your break from busy so that you can decrease your rushing and increase your equanimity and sense of joy. You'll find that each time you implement one, you'll feel more confident, self-assured, and in charge of your emotional responses.

> "If everything is important, then nothing is."
> — Patrick Lencioni

• The Solutions •

This is where you merge the power of conscious thinking with deliberate action, creating positive change in a way that only you can make happen. Now that you've worked through the mindfulness practices and have kindled a new way of thinking, you'll be more likely to readily adopt these practical solutions with greater ease and success. Each solution will help you curb, and even change, behaviors and habits that may undermine your busy-free goals. It's time to rock and roll and have some fun with making busy a thing of the past as you consciously choose your daily state of being.

Descheduling

Descheduling is another form of editing your time and managing your days. Descheduling your calendar opens space to expand your well-being instead of extending the timeline of your day. These descheduling tips are practical ways to reduce, or at least illuminate, the extraneous and gratuitous items that continually find their way onto your calendar.

When accepting invitations or volunteering to manage additional responsibilities, take a few minutes and check in with what you're feeling inside before jumping into something new. By being aware of the importance you've attached to your obligations, you'll be able to organize your calendar in a way that will feel more satisfying and less stressful.

Use these descheduling tips to set you up for the edits you want to make to your schedule. And before adding anything new, ask yourself: *Which events do I find myself dreading and which events do I cancel more often than I attend?* The answers to both provide valuable insight to your motivations and will help you determine whether you put that obligation on your calendar.

The Solution

- *Hit the pause button.* Take time to respond! Imagine a big pause button directly in front of you. Hit it, and stop the clock before you respond to invitations, situations, or criticism.

- *Know when to arrive and when to leave.* Staying too long at the party makes it tough to get up the next morning. This is as much a metaphor as it is a practice. When participating in an event, set a plan prior to attending; without one, we often do things we wouldn't have done if we had thought things through. Protect your schedule by choosing your invitations with your big picture in mind and by asking yourself those two questions in this solution's introduction.

- *Make an appointment for you to be yourself.* This is so important, because you're not optional. Schedule your time, color-code it, and be sure that you view it as an appointment, not as a placeholder that can be shifted for someone or something else. Remember, "If everything is important, then nothing is."

- *Listen to your intuition.* That little voice inside is usually right. Pause and listen when it speaks to you. Trust it, and your intuition will guide you in your right direction.

- *Space out.* Giving yourself space will open up your creativity, stimulate problem-solving, enhance your ability to relax, and give you the clarity to discover a passion.

Coding Your Calendar

Take stock of your calendar by coding your engagements "Must," "Want," and "Just Because."

- *Musts* are the obligations that better both your life and the lives of your loved ones. They might not always fill you up in the moment, but they are part of your big picture. They are the components that keep your life moving forward, not in a frenzied and chaotic way but in a direction that will support your growth, safety, and the quality of your life and of others'.

- *Wants* are where we can get sideswiped, since we have to know what we need before we can determine what we want. Review the Need/Want Connection on page 38, and build your wants into your calendar based on that formula.

- Your *Just Becauses* should always fill you up. These are the actions you take to invigorate your creativity, stimulate your imagination, and expand your soul connection with yourself and your joyful connection with others.

- Now take a look at your calendar; is there a workable balance between your Musts, Wants, and Just Becauses? When you look at your calendar, do you feel satisfied? If not, adjust your calendar now. Edit one Must, Want, or Just Because at a time. Next week, edit one more, and keep editing until you find an integration among the three that feels right to you. The new you. The less busy you.

Coding your calendar can be a real eye-opener and a quick tool for establishing day-to-day descheduling. Eliminate or decrease your calendar-crowders one at a time, and over time, you'll have more time for Just Becauses.

Healthy No

If you're operating from an *everything-is-important* point of view, then this is the solution for you. Self-monitoring, editing, and learning to deliver a healthy no, as touched on earlier, is vital to living a less crowded and more vibrant life.

Many women are not taught how to approach and engage in healthy disagreements, and this can intensify the fear surrounding conflict. *No* is an honest sentiment and one that often helps others understand what is expected and permissible. It is absolutely necessary in editing your choices. Delivering a *slow yes* and a *fast no* takes practice, just like anything else.

If you're uncomfortable saying no, begin by saying a small and safe no to invitations and events that won't dramatically impact you. Use the Super Solutions Process to dig under your discomfort when saying no.

No for Novices

Growing up, I was taught to never begin a sentence with the word *no*. Later I was taught that *no* is a complete sentence. So, which one is it? It's both! Here are some ways to get comfortable with adding and communicating this simple yet powerful word.

- *Mirror, mirror.* Get used to saying no by saying it to your mirror. Think of an upcoming situation in which you do not want to participate. First, think of what you want to do, and with that in mind, practice saying no. Looking into the mirror, say no at least five times every day until you can express your healthy no with confidence and compassion.

- *Softeners.* These are the words we wrap around messages when we feel those messages will be difficult for others to hear. In this case, your no is probably more difficult for you to hear than it is for the person receiving it. Avoid the words *but* and *however* as often as possible because everything you say before these words will be discounted or diminished. If possible, begin your no answer with a sincere thank-you and a compliment. Here are some examples: (1) Using *and*: I'd love to help you. I'm already committed that day and I need to say no. (2) Using *thank-you* and a compliment: Thank you for asking; I'm sure the event will be spectacular. I'm already committed that day and need to say no.

- *Begin with* I. Using *I* instead of *you* is a strong and positive communication technique. Using *you* often makes others feel blamed or attacked and puts them on defense, and it's difficult to be in a collaborative or understanding frame of mind when we feel either. To help your message of no be heard, and to avoid follow-up questions that can be stressful (such as, "Why not?"), try to use *I* rather than *you* whenever possible. For example: "I can't today, I have a lot on my plate," rather than, "I can't today; you should have asked me earlier."

Saying no gives someone else the opportunity to say yes and experience the role of giving. Helping others is admirable, unless you do it so often that you become frustrated and overwhelmed. That's when you know it's necessary to set better boundaries and deliver your healthy no. Boundaries are important to all relationships, including the one we have with ourselves. No second-guessing or confusion: just a good healthy limit for good healthy living.

Taming Time

Time is like a two-year-old: if we don't manage it consistently, it will wreak havoc on everything in its path. You can tame your time by using this practical solution and applying it to the basic aspects of daily living. Acknowledging your preference and clearly communicating your need and desire for assistance will guide you in protecting and maintaining the quality of your time.

The Solution

1. *Clear the clutter.* As a metaphor for clutter, think of a flower garden: a plant will not produce beautiful flowers if it's crowded by other plants. It needs the breeze to move under and around it, oxygenating it for growth. Our lives are similar. Without the room to think and rest, we can't sustain our creativity, sense of peacefulness, or productivity. Clearing the clutter will generate space everywhere, including in your mind. Clutter is a distraction and impedes our sense of relaxation and imagination. Even the clutter that you can't

see, that's behind a closed door, say, has an impact on your emotional and mental well-being; you know it's there even if you are not looking at it. For things to grow — ideas, solutions, artful endeavors, skills, and successes — space is required on all planes: spiritual, intellectual, and practical. This solution will help you choose one type of clutter to clear each day.

- Set a timer, and give yourself five or ten minutes to begin the process of decluttering.

- Remove it, don't just move it. Touch an object once, and decide to keep it, toss it, or repurpose it. If you find yourself going back and forth on whether to keep a certain item even though you haven't used it for six months or more, it's probably time for it to go. We all have those items in our closets, on our desks, in the rooms of our houses. Pick one area at a time, and refresh the space by editing out the items that are waiting to find a new home.

- Donate. Use the one-year rule. If something remains untouched, unworn, or unused for a year, then it's time to repurpose or donate it.

2. *Know your likes and dislikes.* If you're not clear on your likes and dislikes, you'll end up dreading how you spend your time. For example, if you don't like to cook, don't plan an elaborate dinner. If you like to leave work on time, be mindful of what conversations and projects you begin during

the last hour of your day. Be as mindful with your day-to-day likes and dislikes as you are with serious and long-term choices. Use the reminders below to make swift and sensible time-decluttering choices:

- Editing time clutter is easier when you are mindfully aware of what brings you pleasure. Refer to the two questions in the Descheduling section on page 132 as a quick audit to determine the balance between importance and pleasure a particular task or obligation brings.

- Honor your values; they will inform your choices, if you let them.

- Consistently tap into your natural attributes for guidance when making choices that remove the time clutters that are holding you back.

TIPS FOR YOUR HOME LIFE

- Prepare your next-day routine the night before.

- If you have trouble getting up in the morning, place your alarm clock across the room the night before so you'll have to get up to turn it off. That will keep you from hitting the snooze button!

- Take advantage of online ordering. Have ingredients in your pantry, freezer, and cupboard that you can combine with fresh ingredients at the last minute. I call this your Magic Meals:

on-hand ingredients for three of your go-to easy family meals.

Tips for Your Professional Life

- *Keep your desk at work.* In other words, don't take your work home with you if at all possible. Of course, there are times when this can't be avoided; however, make it the exception, not the practice. Research by economist John Pencavel of Stanford University shows that our productivity drops after a "50-hour work week." And with 40 percent of us working more than fifty hours a week and another 20 percent of us working more than sixty, we all need to make the decision to *keep work at work*, since doing so is better for our productivity and our health.

- *Stay on topic.* Relationships in the workplace are important and can offer a more rounded and enjoyable work experience. Building strong relationships and finding common ground with colleagues can enhance your overall professional life. However, try to avoid getting too chummy with office mates, since it can interfere with your productivity at work and impact your decision making when difficult choices arise. Avoid watercooler gossip, and stay on task as much as possible; doing so will make leaving your desk behind easier and increase your productivity under that fifty-hour cutoff.

3. *Delegate.* Concise and clear communication is needed for successful delegating. Use the below outline to organize your delivery and to stay on track:

- State what you need using the *I* message outlined in the Healthy No solution on page 137.

- Express to the person you are delegating to how her help will make a difference.

- Provide a clear outline of the task, including when you need it completed.

- Make a positive statement that represents the best of that person's attributes and how they contribute to the goal at hand: "I know you'll do a terrific job with this task because you are very organized and creative."

- Ask if she has any questions and answer accordingly.

- Finish with a brief recap for each of the bullet points above and, if appropriate, send a thank you email recapping your conversation. Clear and concise communication saves time. When people know what's expected of them they are more likely to meet those expectations and feel good about doing so.

4. *Stay in your lane.* Be clear of what lane you are in and stay out of others'. Solving problems by overhelping does not help; rather, it encumbers

individual contribution and commitment. Frequent lane switching is a time zapper, since often the same thing gets done by multiple players. Evaluating and modifying where needed, and frequently visiting the intentions behind your actions, will help to anchor you in your own lane.

Count Your Yessings

Are you in the overscheduling habit of saying yes to most everything? Do you find that your list of to-dos doesn't get done because the things you've given a spontaneous yes to get moved to the top of that list? If this sounds familiar, counting your yessings is the way to break this busy habit.

This solution raises your awareness to what and how often you are automatically agreeing to do something or be somewhere. The steps involve conscious thinking so that you can mindfully choose to edit the time-zapping commitments that don't line up with your Need/Want Connection (page 38) or ensure the balance of your Must-Wants-Just Becauses outlined in Coding Your Calendar on page 134.

The Solution

1. When you say yes to something that is not a part of your planned schedule for the day, count how many times in one day by making a mental note, or recording it on your phone or on a piece of paper.

2. Be mindful of the feelings that stir inside (anxiety,

guilt, insecurity, uneasiness). Don't judge your feelings; just be aware of and observe them.

3. At the end of the day, and before you go to bed, count your number of yessings from the day.

4. Remove from your list all the yessings that caused you to feel anxious or tense. What's left is tomorrow's yes list. Removing those yessings is a vital step in initiating change.

5. The next day, each time you say yes, remove a yes from your list. Once you have used up all your yessings, that's your signal to stop saying yes for the day. You've now established the number of yessings that feels right for you, give or take one or two.

To take this one step further, on the following day, first thing, remove one yessing from your newly established list. Test out the new number of yessings and see if you feel even better. If so, make that your new number.

Take a few quiet moments and reflect on the message behind your yessings, and with practice, you'll become more aware of which yessings feel agreeable, and the act of giving will become a conscious pleasure rather than an unconscious obligation.

There are always times when it's necessary to be open and ready to help those in need. Practicing the yessing technique is not meant to close you off to those situations; rather, it is a method for setting healthy boundaries, living more consciously, and producing balance in your daily lifestyle.

> *"People will forget what you said, people will forget what you did, but people will never forget how you made them feel."*
> — *Maya Angelou*

Flip

As we know by now, it's all in how we look at things. Unforeseen difficulties or unexpected circumstances can catch us so off guard that we react out of fear and confusion rather than responding with calm and confidence. Once fear gets rolling, adrenaline starts pumping through our body, clouding our ability to think clearly and search for solutions. We rely on familiar habits to get us through the situation, and we feed the fear and frustration by continually restating the problem, thereby limiting the possibility of seeing the situation from a different perspective.

Successfully facing life's unexpected curveballs has everything to do with attitude and perspective. If you can quell fear, your brain will operate more effectively, lighting up the region that is involved in problem-solving and managing emotion. An *I can* attitude is essential; since we often base our actions on our expectations, why not expect the best outcome? We'll be more likely to see opportunities if we're looking for them.

Doing the Flip will help you shift your view so that you can change your verbal interpretation of the situation from problem to opportunity. By changing the words you use to recount an experience, you change your focus, expanding your view of what is possible. When we stand on a beach and look out at the ocean, we see one view. But if we stand on a cliff high above the ocean, our view is vastly more abundant. It's that step back that we often need to change our perspective, and doing the Flip helps you do that.

If you feel uncertain or skeptical about this solution, be sure to read my story at the end of the exercise. Using the Flip made all the difference to me in getting through a tough time, and I hope it does the same for you. Even if you're doubtful of the Flip statement you created in the beginning, simply having the intention to improve your circumstances will help you to assimilate your words and reinforce your actions — and change will abound.

Being aware of how you talk to yourself invites your awareness to do the talking.

The Solution

1. *Problem statement.* Write one sentence, as outlined in the Super Solutions Process, page 83.
2. *Flip the statement.* Turn the problem into the solution. You will find a list of Flip words at the end of this exercise.

   Situation: I can't lose weight. It's just too hard, and I don't have the time.
   Flip: I have the opportunity to lose weight. It is a challenge that I'm prepared to master.

   Situation: I'm afraid my relationship is ending. I feel lost and I'm questioning whether I should stay.

Flip: I'm motivated to rediscover what I want in my relationship. I'm curious about what I need.

Situation: I hate it when this happens to me. I never get a break.

Flip: I'm open to the opportunity that is before me. It's just for me, and I will use it to transform.

3. *Repeat and defeat.* By repeating your Flip statement, you will defeat the negative vibe of your old thinking. Use your Flip statement to reinforce what you want and as a mantra to remind you of your goal. Repeat it first thing in the morning, and as often as you can throughout the day. And at the end of your day, let it be your last thought before turning out the lights at night.

MY FLIP

In 2012, two days before Christmas, the building my business was located in was flooded by a severe storm, and suddenly we were up to our shins in water. My business partner and I lost hundreds of thousands of dollars in the improvements we had made, most of them just one year earlier. We were devastated by the loss, but not for long. We made a conscious choice to look at the misfortune as an opportunity in disguise. We immediately began focusing on what we could do to move us toward what we wanted. We considered options that were now available to us, such as relocating to a building that was less costly, remodeling again with even better improvements, and redefining our business model to reflect our desire to enjoy more of life outside work. Our loss meant that contractors *would reap the benefits of a new remodeling job. The movers who moved our studio and the owners of the new building all benefited from our experience. By looking at our situation this way, we saw our new circumstances as unexpected opportunities for so many beyond ourselves. We consciously chose to see it as an adventure of the unknown, a balancing of loss and gain. It was this attitude that allowed us to focus on building rather than tearing down. It was not without challenge or hardship. Throughout the adventure, we used our flip statement to maintain a clear view of what we chose to see, and that kept us focused and inspired. The day of the flood, I gave this process the acronym **FLIP: F**ind **L**ight and **I**nspiration in the **P**roblem. We did, and you will, too!*

Situation Words	FLIP Words
challenge	opportunity
fear	motivation
sacrifice	offer
loss	discovery
alone	independent
unknown	adventure
questioning	curiosity
failure	success
mistakes	learning
disappointment	evolution
change	transform
hate	love
never	sometimes
happens	choice
blocks	stepping stones

Using these Flip words distinctly changes your interpretation of a situation, which assuredly changes your outcome. Once you get into the habit of doing the Flip, you'll regularly use it to make certain and positive change.

Setting Healthy Boundaries

Constant availability, unyielding accommodation of others, and unrealistic expectations can easily morph into time-zapping habits. Busy has no boundaries; you just keep going and going. It's like treading water with no shore in site — you keep doing it in hopes that someone will show up and rescue you. If this sounds familiar, it's time to set some new boundaries.

Boundaries are not designed to keep others out; rather, they're meant to protect personal space so that each of us can develop, protect, and maintain our sense of self. Setting healthy boundaries is fundamental in maintaining healthy relationships and personal well-being. Most people understand this and respect the boundaries that we set. However, if we have not established consistent boundaries, others won't have a clue as to when they are crossing them. When this happens, frustration and anger are often the result, pushing us over the line of our ill-set boundaries. Understanding your limits before you reach them will help you set good boundaries and give you the confidence to enforce them. You may get pushback from others when you set new boundaries; this is often a reaction to the changing dynamics that new boundaries bring. Setting and enforcing boundaries comes with a learning curve, and once you get on the other side of that, you'll be in a better position to manage your time.

The Solution

1. *Flag your feelings.* Be aware of feeling resentful or uncomfortable. These feelings are likely signals that you've reached the limits of the boundary you have set. A yellow flag means pause and evaluate. Evaluate whether you really need to do what's being asked of you. Is it too close to a limit that you've set for yourself? Or is there some way you could modify the situation or request so that you feel more comfortable? A red flag means stop and communicate. A red flag is a sure sign that you have reached your limit and that it's time to communicate that. Be firm and kind while clearly stating why you won't accept whatever is causing you the discomfort, and follow it by restating your boundary and what you will accept.

2. *Review your Need/Want Connection.* Determine what you need to get done before you accept any requests from others. Be sure you really have the time to do what's being asked without it affecting your positive mood.

3. *Use clear communication.* Don't beat around the bush when you express a boundary. Do be mindful of the relationship you have with the other person and the style in which she communicates. Doing so will make what you have to say easier for her to hear. And that's key in getting

your point across in a direct and compassionate manner.

4. *Keep it simple.* Don't overthink whether or not you should do something — go with your gut!

5. *Consistency is key.* Establish healthy boundaries by sticking to them. Those around you will stop expecting so much when you stop doing so much.

Think of boundaries as the handrails on a staircase; everyone feels better when they're there.

Mind Your Mantra

Mantras are power words and have long been a method for subduing incessant distracting thoughts. In the Buddhist and Hindu traditions, mantras have profound spiritual significance. In Western culture, we often use mantras as we would a business's tagline. This is not in any way meant to diminish the sacred importance or meaning; it is simply a practical method of engaging your thinking and your awareness. Mantras are another tool for staying focused on the big picture and arming you against unwanted diversions.

The Solution

1. *Create.* Create a four- to six-word phrase — stated in the positive — of what you need or want. For help with this, use the Whittling technique on page 85.

2. *Repeat.* Repeat your mantra at least three times a day and whenever you need a nudge to stay

focused on your big picture. If you are getting ready for a situation, event, or presentation and you need an extra boost of confidence, repeating your mantra will help you stay on task.

3. *Make it happen.* Write your mantra on a piece of paper, and slip it into your pocket or purse. Stick it on your bathroom mirror, fridge, or car console. See it, believe it, and make it happen!

Here are a few of my favorite mantras:

- *Honor thy thoughts.* This keeps my mind from getting caught up in distracting thoughts.

- *Do it right now, not forever.* I use this when I start talking myself out of doing something I know is good for me, like exercising or skipping the chips.

- *Focus on what I want.* This keeps negative thoughts out and directs my energy toward my desired outcome.

- *Listen, not judge.* This mantra helps when I find myself being judgmental about another's reasoning, actions, or thoughts.

- *TIME — To Immediately Mind the Experience.* This one is helpful when I'm allowing distractions in and I'm not open, available, and present to my family and loved ones.

The Artful Ask

There's nothing to lose in asking for help, but there is a lost opportunity when you choose not to ask. When we help others, we feel better. Being helpful is a guiding principle for healthy living, and its benefits reach much farther than just the immediate act of helpfulness. Helpfulness triggers our feel-good hormones, stimulating blood flow and reducing stress hormones, tension, and anxiousness.

Many of us forget that our overly helpful nature may be preventing others from taking on the helping role. And, in the case of our children, when we do too much for them, we rob them of the opportunity to develop their helpful character and build their compassion. If you are always in the helpful mode, when will others have the opportunity to feel good about lending a helping hand?

Opening a door for someone, holding the elevator, and letting someone change lanes in traffic are simple ways we can practice helpfulness. But what about asking others to help you?

The Solution

- Do you often feel if you don't do it, no one else will?
- Do you believe that if someone else performs a task, it won't be done the way you want it to be?
- Is it easier for you to do what needs to be done than it is to ask someone else for help?
- At the end of the day, do you often feel like you can't depend on anyone for help?
- Is this statement true?: "No one ever offers to help me."

If you answered yes to most of these questions, you're an excellent helper. It's likely that others aren't helping because they see you're just fine doing it yourself. If you're not clear on why it's difficult for you to ask for help, return to the Super Solutions Process on page 83 and work the five steps on page 87. Once you've got a more well-defined answer as to why it's difficult to ask for help, move to the next step of this solution.

1. *Develop the art of the ask:*
   - State what you need.
   - State how it will help you. Be specific.
   - State what unique quality or ability the helper brings to the situation.
   - State how he will benefit from helping.
   - State what your preferred outcome will look like.

2. *Create a mantra.* The above five statements frame the mantra you use for asking. Having a mantra reminds you to stay in the moment, solidifies the importance of the ask, and helps you to stay on track when asking.

3. *Build the habit.* Feeling uncomfortable when asking is normal. After all, our mind's asking muscles are out of shape. You've got to build them up, just as you would your biceps. The more often you practice, the easier it will become.

The artful ask is a busy-busting habit that will benefit you in many ways. For one, it can build a partnership between the one asking and the one offering. When people work together toward the same goal, a sense of unity prevails. Time can be both saved and shared!

> *I'm not in your rush.*

Rate the Rush

If you find yourself adding too much to your day with frequency, then it's time to reassess, rethink, and reboot. The solution below will help you do just that. You'll determine whether or not you need to be rushing and how much it might be stealing your day. You'll restart your day at any point and get back on track quickly, and without rushing.

The Solution

1. *Reassess.* Take a one-minute break from rushing, and reassess the importance of your pace:
   - Is it really necessary?
   - Is it life threatening if I don't _____?
   - Is it ego threatening and I'll feel _____ if I don't _____?
   - What's the worst thing that can happen if I stop rushing?
   - What's the best thing that can happen if I stop rushing?
2. *Rethink.* Do I want the worst thing or the best thing to happen? Ask yourself this question to help bring your desire to a more conscious level of your thinking.

3. *Reboot.* Now you're ready to restart your day, with your clear direction in front of you. Fill in this sentence: I want _____, and the best thing is _____, and that's what I choose for me today.

Rushing Reminders

- What doesn't get done today will be waiting for you tomorrow.
- Practice the artful ask, and see if something can get done by someone else.
- You can reprioritize and move the task to another time, or you can let go of it altogether.
- Rate whether or not it's worth the rush one situation at a time; doing it this way will make it feel more manageable to adopt the solution and turn it into a time-saving habit.

● Take Five

Another great way to get the busy out of your day is to take five minutes to redirect the moment. You'll be impressed at how it's just enough to get you back on track and out of the busy lane.

The Solution

1. *Breathe.* Begin by taking five deep breaths in through your nose and out through your mouth.

2. *Be quiet.* Repeat silently, "I'm quieting my mind and thoughts so that I can hear my solution voice."

3. *Actively redirect.* Give yourself three reasons you need and want to stop what you are doing or thinking.

4. *Your redirect statement.* I'm choosing to redirect my day because _____ is more important/satisfying/lasting.

5. Repeat your redirect statement five times.

6. Return to your day with this new direction guiding your choices.

7. Repeat your redirect statement as often as needed.

Turning Off

Do you daydream? Do you gaze up at the sky just to enjoy its presence? Do you take a walk just to be in nature? Do you sit and eat without the TV on or computer open? Or do you grab your phone in the morning before you hug your partner? Do you check social media more often than you check in with your spouse or kids? Do you ever turn off all your electronics, even for an hour? Do I sound crazy for even suggesting any of this? Perhaps. But it's time to consider what all this turning on is doing to your health, your sense of calm, and your daily schedule.

The average amount of time spent on social media is nearly two hours a day, give or take thirty minutes. Sadly, as reported in a 2014 *New York Times* article, we spend on average a mere nineteen minutes a day reading — I hope you're spending the full amount with this book!

When your mind is crowded, there is no room for imagination, joy, and peace. Kicking back for ten or fifteen minutes to *just be* can calm your mind and make space for creativity, problem-solving, and an improved ability to focus. It's also quite likely that you'll feel refreshed and more energetic afterward. The sound of silence is a natural wellness elixir, a nutrient-rich mind-body break. It's essential to give yourself permission to be quiet and unplug and equally important to share the value of unplugging with your loved ones. You'll clear your thoughts, open your mind, refresh your energy, and see new ways of increasing the quality of your day — all of which will save you time and boost your mood.

The Solution

1. *Disconnect.* Set a time each day for no electronics. If you're highly addicted to them, begin with two or three minutes each day and move up a little bit each week until you are at twenty minutes or more. It also helps to establish unplug-always zones. For example, decide to have no gadgets at meals and at bedtime. Turn off your phone, laptop, and tablet when you turn in for the night.

2. *Connect.* Honor your physical and spiritual-minded self by going for a walk, sitting and thinking, meditating, or gardening. Notice how

you feel when you are not distracted by your phone and other electronics. You will remember conversations more clearly and recall moments more vividly, and at the end of the day those experiences will play a role in your connection with body, mind, spirit, and soul.

3. *Redirect.* Now it's time to redirect your energy with this simple fifteen-minute restorative pose. In the first seven or so minutes, your heart rate will find a rhythmic and reduced pulse, signaling the body to relax. Elevating your legs will stimulate the return blood flow from the feet to the heart and help stimulate blood flow throughout the body. This refreshed blood flow is a cellular restoration, and you'll feel relaxed and refreshed afterward.

- Lying supine, prop your legs over the seat of a chair or stack of pillows.
- Knees should be higher than your head and feet slightly higher than your knees.
- Legs and knees should be bent at a 90-degree angle and hip distance apart.
- Close your eyes and relax your arms by your sides.
- Breathe in through your nose and exhale out your mouth for fifteen minutes. Keep your focus on your breath.

- Take this revitalized time to really engage with the here and now.

The constant use of electronics can provide a false sense of importance, increase the tension of busyness, and bolster habits of distractions. A phone is a piece of technology, not a best friend. Remind yourself to unplug, and reconnect with the breath of life.

Here you are! How does it feel? You've swung open the doors, exposed your busy habits, and invited in a new approach to living. You're now prepared to enjoy your life with more freedom and less pressure to perform. We continue to influence other women, generations before us and after us, each time we enjoy our leisure without labeling it as lazy and affirm that doing less can be more rewarding than the recognition that comes with performing. Remember to appreciate yourself for who you are, not for what you do. These real-life solutions and practices are your methods for doing just that.

Keep this book close by, and if your days rev up and accelerate back into a busy pace, pull it out and jump into a solution or mindful practice instead of jumping back into busy. The next chapter is exactly what will help you stay on the path to doing that. Fifty-two busy-free reminders await you and will take you through an entire year, one mindful thought and busy-free day at a time!

CHAPTER NINE

Your Busy-Free Playbook
Refreshers and Reminders

This chapter will take you to the next level of busy-free living. It's essentially a cheat sheet that you can laminate and put on your wall, nuggets that will help keep you on track. Whether you've mastered the practices and solutions or you feel as though they're just beginning to sink in, these refreshers and reminders will help stoke your new perspective so that you don't slip back into your old habits. Just like one of the many drops that make the waterfall or the first step up the mountain, a single action helps get you where you want to go, and when you add your phenomenally powerful thinking into the equation, you'll maintain your pace without jumping back into the race. You're in charge. You have the skills, attributes, and know-how for staying in the right mind-set, and these power pauses will remind you that making just one small adjustment in how you spend your time can make a big difference in how you live your life. They are the CliffsNotes of busy-free living!

Without further ado, here are fifty-two refreshers and reminders for a weekly (or even daily) audit, designed to support everything you've already learned from this book. They'll give you a mindful boost and a vibrant revival to your week. Have fun!

1. *Adopt a latitude attitude.* Attitude is everything! Have you ever noticed how your mood instantaneously shifts when you start talking about a vacation you're planning or leaving for? That's the latitude attitude: just thinking about being on vacation helps everything feel better. It's a time-saving way to reduce stress and to release the mental pressure of having to get stuff done. This week, if you can get away for a mini-vacation, do it! Make one day this week special by planning an outing just for fun. Plan it as you would any vacation, even if it's just an hour getaway! And if you can't physically go away, simply get your mind into a latitude attitude, and you just might discover somewhere you actually never thought about going to. When you return from that mental refresher you'll feel better about tackling what's in front of you; a better attitude will help you be more productive, positive, and prepared. So grab your sandals and your sunblock. It's time to take a break and get into the attitude that restores your energy and sense of fun.

2. *Be curious and inspired.* For this reminder, focus on honoring your time with curiosity and inspiration. If you're not curious about something, or it doesn't feel inspiring, don't add it to your schedule! Curiosity can spark

imagination, memory, and learning. Your brain's hippo-campus lights up like a neon sign and releases the feel-good chemical dopamine. All this just by being curious! And feeling inspired can move you from indifference to optimism. It's easier to problem-solve and manage daily stressors when you're in a curious and inspired frame of mind. It's difficult to be judgmental if you're curious, or apathetic if you're inspired. Be and look for what inspires you — it will transform the way you experience your world.

3. Find that Friday state of mind. Research shows that tak-ing a day off is good for your health. When you feel bet-ter, you'll be better. The key is to plan the day off, not to end up getting so run-down that you have to call in sick at work, leaving coworkers to pick up the slack. By planning a day off, you're free from guilt or the worry that you are doing something that is unethical or unfair to others. You can plan what day you take off and prepare your team in advance, and, if needed, you can arrange to work additional hours to make up for the loss in in-come. If you hear yourself saying, "I don't have time to take a day off," that's a flashing red light that you really do need one! Maybe you can't take the whole day off, and if that's the case, organize an early-day departure so that you have a few hours to rejuvenate by doing some-thing that is not a necessity. The anticipation alone will boost your mood as you lead up to your Friday state of mind.

4. *Meditate to activate.* Meditation lowers blood pressure, eases chronic pain and anxiety, boosts your mood and immune system, and stimulates the region of your brain that's involved in creative problem-solving and managing emotion and behavior. When you meditate you activate your resourceful thoughts, which will help keep you on track. Sometimes all we need is a one-minute mental reboot to stay focused and out of busy traps. Set aside one minute, or revisit the Meditation Magic for a mindful reboot. Once in the morning and again at night may be all that you need to refresh your mind and actively extinguish distracting thoughts.

5. *Set your tempo.* Acknowledge your pace, and commit to letting go of one busy habit today. Slow down — you're worth it.

6. *See your big picture.* You get to decide how your life looks. However it looks, it will reflect your choices. Begin today with a quick review of your big picture, asking yourself, "What do I need to get what I want?" Then take one action every day to move you in that direction. You may not get there by the end of the day, or the week, but you'll be a lot closer, and a lot clearer, and you will likely be filled with a sense of satisfaction and confidence.

7. *Set priorities.* Today, remind yourself to balance the time you spend on your projects with the priorities of your big picture. Is it necessary or needed? How will it make a difference in my day if I pass on doing it? Take

one minute for each question, and then make a decision that fits your priorities.

8. State your intention. None of us wants to be like a hamster on a wheel, running in circles. Time is too precious to spin around and not make progress. You can avoid that spinning by setting your intention before taking action. Doing so is instant TLC for your consciousness; it's a mindful practice with an emphasis on purposeful action. Words with intention can propel your behaviors and choices in an effective and positive manner. Mindfully affirm your intention before making decisions by asking yourself two questions: "What is my intention for this action?" and "How do I want to feel after I take this action?" Your purpose will harness your thoughts and propel you toward what you want. No more running in circles!

9. Connect with nature. Nature asks for nothing, and yet it is fully present to us. Pets offer the same loving connection. Take time today to appreciate the earth, the sky, the breeze, and the animals that bring unconditional love and balance to the ecosystem we all inhabit.

10. Listen to your heart. Place your hand over your heart, and listen, especially if you are struggling with a decision. Clear your head of any thoughts with five deep inhales and exhales. Then allow your heart to speak. Feel what your heart has to say rather than thinking from your head. Practice listening to your heart, for it will always speak the truth.

11. *Disconnect to reconnect.* Disconnecting from distractions and reconnecting with love, joy, and peace is an essential way to nurture your inner power. Mindfully share time with one person in your inner circle at least once today, or this week, for fifteen minutes. Remind yourself to keep the conversation light and fun. And leave electronics out of it. We stimulate our love hormone oxytocin when we see and hear the people we love, a phenomenon that doesn't happen with an email or text. You'll feel great after your connection. Your energy will be uplifted, and you'll be more ready to focus on the positive.

12. *Expect the unexpected.* Life unfolds, and as it does, the unexpected often appears. Having the right mind-set is your best tool for turning any panic or chaos brought about by the unexpected into prospects for change. Choose to focus on what you want, not on what you fear. Doing so will direct your attention to solutions, no matter what may be in front.

13. *Tap out.* For today, stay out of things that don't need you. If you are not essential to the situation, tap out and stay out. Retire from being the family therapist, and allow others to figure things out for themselves. This week, take a break from mediating, whether it's a battle of will between two coworkers or an argument between family members. Let others hash it out, and if they ask, "Why didn't you help me?" let them know, "I knew you could handle it!" You're not giving up on anyone; you're

getting out of the way. Tapping out lets you tap into how you feel without another person's mess.

14. *Say it like you mean it.* If you want something, say what you want. If you need something, say what you need. The best way to get your needs and wants met is to be clear about what you're asking for and then framing the request with "I need" instead of "You should." "You should" statements put others on the defense rather than in a place of cooperation. And don't forget the intention behind the request. Intention drives the energy of your words and the tone of your delivery. Say it like you mean it, and say it with kindness. Saying it like you mean it saves a lot of time and avoids time-zapping misunderstandings that distract you from your big picture.

15. *Look up.* It is difficult to frown when you look up. Just by looking up, you can change your perspective on a situation. When faced with frustration, look up and smile. And don't underestimate the power of your smile. A genuine, heartfelt smile has the power to lighten up a situation, defuse tension, and increase a sense of happiness and cooperation. It may be just the pause you need to see what you may have missed as well as an invitation to dynamically and positively engage with another.

16. *Connect with others.* Is the time you're spending enriching the quality of the experience and the relationship, or are you multitasking your moments? If you're going for a run and calling your sister while on your run, neither experience will be fully refreshing, because both activities

will be competing for your brain's attention. We are social beings, and sharing time with others is essential for healthy and vibrant living. But it just doesn't happen when we're splitting moments between connecting one-on-one and doing other things. Plan time to appreciate a loved one, and share the pleasure of each other's company without the gadgets that you know distract you. Take fifteen minutes today to be present with one interaction, conversation, or quiet moment. It will refresh your mind and your connection.

17. Be better, not perfect. Make this your mantra for the week, or the day, and an agreement with yourself for a lifetime.

18. Find your funny bone. If you can find the humor in a situation, when appropriate, of course, it can help defuse conflict, reduce tension, create intimacy, and put things that may have taken a wrong turn in perspective. And it feels good to laugh! Your happy hormones will fire up, and you'll be back on track with a better frame of mind in no time. Keep it light this week, and laugh at least once a day.

19. Breathe deeply. This is my favorite power pause. It's a simple and effective reminder to get in the moment before doing anything else. When you're faced with a challenge or an unexpected situation, pause and take five deep breaths before making a difficult choice, commitment, or change. This will give you just enough time to find your mindful center, rebalance your thinking, and compose your response or action. This technique is powerfully effective and can be a game changer for you in the moment.

20. Say goodbye to multitasking. Our brains don't like multitasking, and it turns out that it doesn't really work, even though it may feel like it does. "Task switching is expensive" and can cost a loss of up to "40 percent of your productivity." This week, start and finish one project before starting another. If you're a hard-core multitasker, start with a task that is small so you can get the feel of finishing it completely. There's only one of you, so match your activities with that in mind.

21. DVR your day. Not every day is a home run; sometimes we're happy just to get to the next base without wiping out. Especially around holidays and special occasions, our days can quickly become overscheduled. Hit your pause button this week, and DVR your day. Think of it as getting to a task later instead of doing it now. One base at a time will get you to home plate. Remember this maxim: How do you eat an elephant? One bite at a time. Keep that in mind, and what doesn't get done now will get done later — or maybe you'll just scratch it off your to-do list altogether.

22. Connect with your senses. Today, plan time for your senses. Give your eyes something beautiful to gaze at, eat something that is delicious and nutritious, take time to experience the fragrance of your garden, listen to an amazing piece of music, and hug someone you love at least eight times. This is a reminder that nurturing your whole body, mind, and spirit is vital for living a busy-free day.

23. *Outsource the nonessentials.* Most successful people are able to get things done. Knowing when to ask for help, and how to ask for it, is absolutely indispensable to accomplishing their goals. They delegate to others, selecting those who are best suited to assist in getting the job done. Today, think of yourself as the CEO of your personal life, and outsource the nonessential tasks, which are anything that doesn't move your goals forward. You may need to let go of control, just a bit, and perhaps the person you ask for help won't do it exactly like you would, but if it's a nonessential, it won't have too much of an impact on the bottom line and could free up some time for you to take a needed break.

24. *Make it a happy hump day.* It's the middle of the week and an opportune time to assess where you're at and what you want the rest of the week to look like. It's also an ideal day to take a midweek break and do something out of your routine that is fun and spontaneous and can shift and refresh your energy and attention. Maybe it's a midweek date with your partner, a movie night at home, or a pajama party with your friend squad. Whatever it may be, use it as a reset your mind-set night, and let that carry you through the rest of the week.

25. *Clear your desk.* Clutter is a barrage of distractions all rolled up in piles here and there. Most of us are pretty

routine about decluttering our homes, but what about what's going on your desk at your office? Clutter creates tension and confusion, significantly affecting our ability to stay focused because our brain interprets it as stuff that needs to get done. This week, when you head into your office, or wherever you encounter clutter, take a few minutes and consider this: Clutter takes energy and physical space. It takes time and thought every time you move it from one place to the next. You put it in a file and then in a drawer; if you forget it's even there, the next move should probably be to the shredder or recycling bin. You can shred and recycle the clutter but not your time. Get your desk clear so your mind can be, too.

26. *Give yourself a time-out.* It's ironic that we set a timer when we cook, when we're doing sports, when we take tests, or when we give a time-out to our kids. It's a very efficient way to get things done, since a set time in which to do something reminds us that there is a beginning and end to everything. That's an important reminder for any OSW, since not setting a stop time is what got us into the busy lane of our lives in the first place. It is time to get off that road and make some space for nothing. Yep, no-thing. Today, give yourself a time-out. Or do it every day this week! It may be ten minutes or thirty, but however long you decide it should be, set the timer and take a mindful recess. In this space you will experience new possibilities, which may be just the answer you've been looking for or the refresher you've needed.

27. *Just say no to surfing.* We all know we shouldn't text while driving, and most of us would prefer that our dinner partners were engaging with us and not their smartphones. According to a recent study, the average person will spend five years of her or his lifetime using social media. Modifying this habit is best accomplished one step at a time. Today, be mindful of when you're using your gadgets. Disengage from using social media while driving, eating, and conversing. Pick all three, or choose one. Can you do it? For a day? Or a week? I think you can. You'll no longer have to wave goodbye to any of those lost years.

28. *Remember my mother's advice.* "It doesn't matter what happens, it only matters how you handle it." This was my mother's repeated advice to me as I was growing up. It is a reminder that our actions and behavior are our choice and not caused by outside events. This liberating philosophy can keep you from getting tangled up in upsetting situations or confrontations. Stay attentive to how you handle yourself, and no matter what is happening you'll be in a better position to proactively resolve the mishap. And, after it passes — and it will — you'll be sure to experience genuine satisfaction in how you handled it.

29. *Be here now.* Stay present. You don't have to do it forever, just for now. If it seems like what you're doing or thinking is too much, it probably is. My mother always said, "Anyone can stand on one leg for a minute but not for a month." Heed that sage and simple advice and pause to assess if your one-legged stance is moving you forward.

30. Play. Playing is a brain pleaser, and when we're having fun our brain releases the feel-good chemical dopamine, as well as pain-masking and stress-busting endorphins. That's part of the appeal of video games and exercise: they stimulate the same two brain chemicals, with exercise probably being the healthier choice of the two. If you feel happier, and experience less stress and pain, you'll be more likely to be active and productive. It can be a rewarding occasion to interact and to expand cooperation, team building, and a refreshing mind-set reset. This week, build in your playtime. It may be a spontaneous dance around the kitchen while cooking (one of my mother's favorites) or a rainy-day scavenger hunt. At the office, collaborate with your team and make one day a month a loony lunch with a stack-the-cups challenge. It really doesn't matter what you do — just have fun! Laugh, keep it light, and remember to play!

31. Choose your words. One of the most powerful ways to change your reality is to mindfully select the words you use to communicate. The key is to get real with what you need to say in a way that gets the results you want, and that begins with your own internal dialogue. When your inner conversation is authentically driving your words, the chances of changing the narrative are better, and that will influence your reality. Having said that, let me be clear: healthy conversations are framed by compassion, kindness, truth, and no judgment. Use that framework to set your intention and dive in with what you have to say. Instead of jumping back and pulling a habitual phrase from your mental filing cabinet, such as "I'm too busy," try changing it up to express more frankly what you need to say, such as "Not right now" or "I'll revisit it at another time." Simple phrases like that can turn your thinking from defense to discoveries and keep you from getting into time-grabbing traps. Try it out today, and be mindful of the healthy framework for creating the message you deliver. Set your intention, take a breath, and state what you have to say in the positive. Avoid passive words such as *maybe* or *I guess so*. Clearly state what you will do now in the moment. You can always revisit it or update it later, and if you feel you need that option, then state that also. "I can do this now, and I will update you at (specific time and date) for what I can do after that." Simple, clear, and concise statements make communication easier and prevent confusion and time-crushing misunderstandings.

32. *Have fun*. How does fun help you allocate more time? Taking a fun break does the same for your mind and body as stepping away from a project; you gain new perspective while increasing your productivity and emotional vitality. Just a few minutes of positive and spontaneous engagement can refresh your outlook and boost your mood. When you place a high priority on your fun factor, your life will feel livelier. Create a moment of fun today, making it a priority, and at the end of the day share that moment with a loved one and let him relive it with you. It will bring a sense of optimism and lighthearted pleasure, both of which can expand your creative problem-solving and lift your spirits.

33. *Spend a guilt-free day.* The term *guilt-free* gets tossed around freely, applied to everything from what we eat to what we think and do. Feeling guilty about what you may have said or done will keep you from moving forward; it's a mental drag that easily zaps your energy. Think of the three things that rouse your guilt. Are they things that you say or do? Just by examining that question, you can bring your relationship with guilt to the surface and begin cultivating mindful solutions for managing it. Owning your mistakes is always necessary for personal growth, as is cutting yourself some slack when you don't meet your own expectations. Today have the attitude of *there's always a next time*. Let that attitude marinate, and use it to help take the sting out of the moment. Recognize your power to repair or improve what has occurred. Doing so will give you hope that the next time will be an opportunity to get it right or at least better.

34. *Dare yourself.* Dare yourself to turn off your phone for a day. Planning it will make it happen! Let everyone know where you are and that you're taking the dare and the day off from the phone. It's a challenge, and you may feel like you're the last one left on earth, but I promise, you'll be amazed with how real your day will feel. You'll see colors more clearly, hear and remember what others say to you, taste food and smell fragrances more richly, and you may just get so relaxed you'll take a snooze. You'll also become acutely aware of just how much time you spend being interrupted by your addiction to the little dare devil in your hands. It constantly dares you to swipe,

tap, browse, and check in. Dare yourself to turn it off, and turn your day on.

35. Tell a story. Approaching your daily schedule as a story puts a playful spin on the day ahead. It lightens the mood when things feel heavy, and it's a creatively effective way to organize the beginning, middle, and end of your day. Edit like a pro, be authentic with your interactions, and clearly communicate in the way you want to be heard. Set your opening scene: What do you plan to finish before noon? Be sure your second act includes a pick-me-up element — something delicious to eat or an enjoyable activity — so that your attention is concentrated and your energy stimulated. And the last act should leave you with anticipation for the end; low-priority tasks that can be done quickly and don't require a great deal of focus are best placed in this part of your day. Let your eagerness for the brilliant ending to your story, your day, fuel your efforts.

36. Reflect. It's easy to let one day carry over into the next and to forget to reflect on the content and events of each day. Reflecting on your day enhances productivity and kindles imagination so you can connect with new ideas and put things into perspective. Reflection is a way to keep your *I-can-get-it-done* mentality in check and absorb what worked and what needs to be adjusted or changed. As American philosopher and psychologist John Dewey espoused, "We do not learn from experience... we learn from reflecting on experience." At the end of each day this week, take a few minutes to reflect on your day, jotting down the strategies that worked best so you can repeat them next time. Give yourself a pat on the back for a day well spent. Experience your moments instead of just letting them pass by.

37. *Be slow.* Make a bold difference today by slowing down. Do one thing at a time; pause and reflect before moving on. Doing so will significantly improve your productivity and mental wellness. Multitasking and its trickery confuse the brain into perceiving everything as important, leading to time-zapping mistakes and misunderstandings. Slowing down increases productivity and positively impacts the quality of your work. Think of it as a delicious soup or sauce; as it simmers the flavors brighten and the taste emerges. That's what happens to your body and mind when you slow down. In broad terms, your thoughts are more nuanced and creative, your imagination more prolific, and your mood and attitude positively enhanced when you stop multitasking and slow down.

38. *Small-chunk.* Taking mindful pauses and using practical time management are ways to small-chunk your way through your day and still get done what you need to without getting overwhelmed. Start with a mindful plan for the day that includes a short, simple sentence stated in the positive that will remind you of today's end goal. Choose the part of the day when you know you are most productive, and use that time for the items requiring the

most focus and time. End your day with a planned reward, one that supports the day's efforts and accomplishments. Use the in-between times for less intensive things on your calendar. Choosing morning, noon, and evening is a common way to divide the day; however, you might want to think of it as morning and midmorning, afternoon and midafternoon, and early evening and after dinner. Whatever you decide, it should be what works for you. It's a time-saving daily scheduling method that gets it done, and rewards you for doing it. You deserve it!

39. Pick progress over perfection. Progress moves you forward, one step at a time. Perfection keeps you stuck, one thought at a time. Those thoughts are often self-critical, getting in the way of new ideas and ambushing your time. It is our flaws and uncertainty that provide space to grow and learn. And as simplistic as that may sound, we often forget that what each day is about is the discoveries we make and the ideas and experiences that flourish because of them. This week, make space for growing and learning, and each time something pops up that needs to be done, be mindfully aware of progressing through the task with an attitude of growing and learning. It will help you step back from the pressure of perfection.

40. Imprint a new blueprint. Your routine may be too, well, routine if you're feeling like you're on autopilot. Feeling flat is a result of wear and tear on your brain and your mind, of doing too much of the same old stuff.

Today, change it up and imprint a new blueprint by switching a few of the day-to-day tasks that feel burdensome or boring. Eat breakfast for dinner, take the scenic route to work rather than the freeway, sit in a different chair at your weekly work meeting, try a new restaurant. Any number of simple changes can reboot your thinking, reestablishing a sense of play and curiosity and awe. Be awed this week by at least one thing, one discovery, one encounter. Make that awe and curiosity part of a new blueprint that redesigns your day.

41. *Refresh your time.* You know those 3:00 PM slowdowns when your energy, enthusiasm, wakefulness, and focus diminish into a disinterested and fatigued slump and everything you're working on comes to a standstill? You need a pick-me-up, and a candy bar is not going to help you; however, these five refreshers can help you sync your mind and body and put you in a better position to finish your day with gusto:

- Get up and move. Change your location, even if it is just a stroll to the company lounge. Take a walk outside and look up; it's a mindful way to get in touch with nature and to remind yourself that you are a part of something vast and astounding.

- Close your eyes for one minute and see the faces of those you love. Send them a smile, and you'll get the same in return.

- Do a power pose. "Adopting expansive postures causes people to feel more powerful." And if you feel more powerful, you'll be more likely to think more effectively.
- Eat something healthy and yummy.
- Drink your water! It is a magic elixir that will hydrate your body and your mind.

42. *Color your plans.* Just because you have things to do doesn't mean you can't make them colorful. Color-coding your calendar is a great organizational tool. You can see at a glance what needs to get done, and the joie de vivre of your week comes alive. It also allows you to see where you've got too much going on and how you can disperse things to even out the flow. Make sure to use your favorite color for the fun — and be sure to get the fun done!

43. *Ask, Why now?* Some days become muddled with plans and demands, and you can lose sight of where you're going and how you're getting there. Revisiting your *why now* can offer a new perspective and help you refocus your direction. Take a few minutes at the beginning of the day, mentally go through your calendar, and ask yourself, *Why now?* If you can't come up with a meaningful answer, take the activity off your schedule and give yourself permission to revisit it later. Throughout the day, when the unexpected pops up and requires your attention or efforts, be sure to ask yourself, *Why now?* before doing anything. Pause to assess before you say yes,

and at the end of the day you won't be at the end of your rope; you'll be ahead of the game!

44. *Pick your trifecta.* Consciously choosing three activities or rituals can be a mindful technique for remaining centered even when unexpected changes intrude on your day. These activities are your trifecta, and they prepare you to end each day with a feeling of victory, that "Yes, I got those three things done." Be sure your trifecta improves your mood, health, and sense of well-being. Mine are meditate, take vitamins, and exercise. Choose three self-care practices that will positively set you up to feel like a winner at the end of the day.

45. *Envision your itinerary.* You might not be able to change your schedule, but you can change how you think about it, and that can alter how you feel about it. Changing your mind-set invites a different perspective and experience. Start your week by looking at it as a travel itinerary instead of a schedule. Think of yourself as traveling through the week; along the way, you'll have sights to see and moments to enjoy. Choose one thing every day that affords you a sense of traveling rather than of the day speeding over you. Set your itinerary, and include points of interest, moments of leisure, and a meal out at least once. At the end of the week you'll look back at where you've been. Instead of reciting what a busy week it was, you'll recapture the moments of where you went and what you saw.

46. Find the me *in* mentor. A mentor directs without leading, encourages without envy, supports without domineering, advocates development and growth, and inspires and motivates self-discovery. Mentorship is an exploration for both the mentor and the mentee. Sometimes life requires that we be our own mentor, trusting our wisdom and gut without the approval or counsel of another. This week, turn within to find the *me* in *mentor*. Be your own advisor, and use your experience and insight to make thoughtful choices that you love and to engage in actions that are deliberate and done with mindful intention. Engage your natural attributes to guide you through uncertainty, and use consideration as a core value in all. Be your best mentor, personal cheerleader, and guru. Trust that you are present and available at any time, as any dedicated mentor is. Take a moment at the top of your day and ask yourself what you will teach and what you will choose to learn. Teaching and learning go together, stimulating and enhancing each other.

47. Begin anew. Hope springs from new beginnings. Releasing the past and unbinding from any grudges, resentments, or misunderstanding frees your psyche to thrive. Start your week with a clean slate, and let go of any grievances, even for a day, and allow your mind to relish fresh ideas, organically quarried solutions, and novel thoughts that encourage creativity and imagination. Your body, mind, and soul will thank you for their refreshed state.

48. Be vibrant. Today can present rich possibilities and unexplored options from which you obtain insight and knowledge about who you are. Knowing what you need and want is essential to knowing who you are, and when you know who you are, you arrive at decisions and solutions more readily and with greater clarity. Today be vibrant, be bold, and be open to all the possibilities that can move you in the direction of discovering your vibrant you. Let that shine emerge, and others will be captivated by and responsive to your glimmer.

49. *Compass your orbit.* Knowing when and how your attributes are directing you lets you consciously access them more frequently, with confident authority and purposeful intent. The attributes you access most help sustain your personal orbit. They direct your actions, maintain your status quo, and compass your reality; like the stars that twinkle and shine in the night's sky, they are what make you extraordinarily you. What are the essentials that make your daily routine manageable and determine your decisions and choices? How do you keep the faith in difficult times? When are your dreams and desires most illuminated? What are the guiding principles that help you navigate each? It may be that you are an ace organizer, a visionary, an optimist, or a pragmatic thinker. Bring those talents and skills front and center today, and let them work for you. Envisioning a standard compass, replace north, south, east, and west with four of your prevalent attributes. This is a strong visual that you can quickly call to mind, especially when life throws a meteor in your direction. You'll be ready, and you'll hit your targeted objective head-on.

50. Add in some big love. What is immensely satisfying, provides great pleasure, and intensely attracts you? What's your big love? Sprinkle your day with some big love by doing something that draws you in and fills you up with spectacular, joyful love. Doing so will be a huge mood booster and a mindful reset to the good things in life. When we're revved up on love and joy, our energy positively shifts, our senses are high-definition, and the day gets remarkably better. Love your day, and spread the sparkle.

51. Get a hobby habit. You may not have known that hobbies deliver a healthy dose of endorphins and are a fun and effective way to produce eustress (pronounced "you-stress"). Eustress is the positive stress that is typically activated while you're on vacation, playing games, or engaging in thrilling adventures like parasailing or ski-ing. The benefits of hobbies don't stop there; they are also known to increase positive thinking and to enhance physical and psychological states, keeping us motivated and enthused about life. Owing to your increased focus, enriched state of mind, and revived enthusiasm, the outcomes of your efforts will likely be more abundant and pleasurable. This week, make a hobby a habit. It's a great break from busy and a nourishing way to sharpen your focus and revitalize your day.

52. Smile and say thank you. A smile and a thank-you are two simple gestures, full of grace and gratitude, that can lift anyone's spirits. When you share your smile and give a heartfelt thank-you, your happiness, and that of others, rises exponentially. Share both today and make your day better and the world a better place, too.

• *In Closing* •

In the course of writing this book, I've had candid and often emotionally revealing conversations with many women of all ages and backgrounds, and I have found that the struggle of *doing it all* and the demands and expectations that lead to busy unite us all. All any of us need do is observe our daughters, our sisters, our friends, and our female coworkers to see how the culture of busy hangs over nearly everything we do. And stepping back to notice how our own busy pace affects the quality of time we spend with our mothers and grandmothers, or other female elders in our lives, is further indication that busy crosses from one generation to the next. My twenty-five-year-old daughter shared something with me regarding this struggle. She said, "Mom, there's no such thing as *finding* time. You can't *make* time. It's not like you can go out and find time hiding in a bush or make time appear; you've got to *plan* time. That's how we can make our lives different, by planning the time to make changes for it to *be* different."

So, from one woman to another, let's plan on making our lives different, framed by our mindful intentions, clear and thoughtful communication, healthy boundaries, and a big dose of love and compassion for one another. Together we make the biggest difference for each one of us and for those who follow after us.

We're not striving for perfect, just better.

Acknowledgments

My band of angels flapped their wings in a continuous harmony of support, faith, love, and humor. Thank you to all of them: My daughter, Juliette, for her insight beyond her years, daily boost, and social media know-how. My business partner and best friend, Jill, for allowing me the time to write this book; never once did she complain about my rambling on about how busy I was writing it! Rebecca, for her counsel and unwavering encouragement and for reminding me of my vision for the book. Roxanne, for her intuition and comic relief. My NLP Master Trainers, Tim and Kris Hallbom, for their brilliant teaching. Dave, for all that I have learned from him and his willingness to thoughtfully answer my numerous questions. And my agent, John Willig at Literary Services Inc., who believed in me first, never gave up on finding a home for my book, and shared with me the true meaning of *ever onward*.

And immense appreciation to New World Library's editorial director, Georgia Hughes, and cofounder, Marc Allen, for providing me this opportunity and giving me not just a home for this book but the invaluable gift of the right home.

Notes

Introduction

Page 7, *I was instantaneously struck*: Tim Hallbom, lecture on the principles of Neurolinguistic Programming Practitioner training, San Francisco, October 2012.

Chapter 3. Giving Busy the Boot

Page 32, *Values, morals, and societal norms*: Dave Grandin, conversation with the author, Menlo Park, March 16, 2017.

Page 33, *A habit consists of*: Charles Duhigg, *The Power of Habit: Why We Do What We Do in Life and Business* (New York: Random House), 19.

Chapter 8. Busy-Busting Solutions

Page 141, *Research by economist John Pencavel*: John Pencavel, "The Productivity of Working Hours," *IZA*, Discussion Paper Series, April 2014; Bob Sullivan, "Memo to Work Martyrs: Long Hours Make You Less Productive," CNBC, January 26, 2015, cnbc.com/2015/01/26/working-more-than-50-hours-makes-you-less-productive.html.

Page 157, *Sadly, as reported in a 2016*: Bijan Stephen, "You Won't Believe How Little Americans Read," *Time*, June 22, 2014, time.com/2909743/americans-reading.

Chapter 9. Your Busy-Free Playbook

Page 169, *"Task switching is expensive"*: Susan Weinschenk, "The True Cost of Multi-Tasking," Brian Wise, *Psychology Today*, September 18, 2012, https://www.psychologytoday.com/blog/brain-wise/201209/the-true-cost-multi-tasking.

Page 172, *According to a recent study, the average person*: David Cohen, "How Much Time Will the Average Person Spend on Social Media During Their Life? (Infographic)," *Adweek*, March 22, 2017, http://www.adweek.com/digital/mediakix-time-spent-social-media-infographic.

Page 176, *As American philosopher and psychologist*: John Dewey, in Tanner Christensen, "Reflection Is the Most Important Part of the Learning Process," 99U, accessed October 30, 2017, http://99u.com/workbook/25481/reflection-is-the-most-important-part-of-the-learning-process.

Page 180, *"Adopting expansive postures causes people"*: Amy Cuddy, in Jesse Singal and Melissa Dahl, "Here Is Amy Cuddy's Response to Critiques of Her Power-Posing Research," *New York Magazine*, September 30, 2016, http://nymag.com/scienceofus/2016/09/read-amy-cuddys-response-to-power-posing-critiques.html.

Recommended Reading

Chopra, Deepak. *Spiritual Solutions: Answers to Life's Greatest Challenges*. New York: Harmony Books, 2012.

Hanson, Rick, and Richard Mendius. *Buddha's Brain: The Practical Neuroscience of Happiness, Love, and Wisdom*. Oakland, CA: New Harbinger, 2009.

Keown, Damien. *Buddhism: A Very Short Introduction*. Oxford, UK: Oxford University Press, 2013.

Kornblatt, Sondra. *Brain Fitness for Women: Keeping Your Head Clear and Your Mind Sharp at Any Age*. Berkeley, CA: Conari Press, 2012.

Index

About the Author

In 2000 Yvonne Tally merged her various healthy living passions and cofounded Poised Inc., a fitness and lifestyle company in the heart of Silicon Valley. As a healthy lifestyle consultant, Yvonne is interested in *what makes people do the things they do*, which led her to become a Neuro-linguistic Programming (NLP) Master Practitioner. This innovative work has allowed Yvonne to help her clients reduce their stress and identify and change their unresourceful habits.

Yvonne speaks and presents to corporations, non-profit organizations, and business and private groups. Her unique blend of knowledge, heart, and wit leaves her clients and audiences with a renewed sense of purpose and cooperation and a refreshed outlook on problem-solving and stress management. She lives in Northern California.

YvonneTally.com

PoisedFit.com